Travels to Hallowed Ground

AMERICAN MILITARY HISTORY
Thomas L. Connelly, Editor

TRAVELS TO HALLOWED GROUND

A Historian's Journey to the American Civil War

By Emory M. Thomas

University of South Carolina Press

Copyright © University of South Carolina 1987

Published in Columbia, South Carolina, by the
University of South Carolina Press

Manufactured in the United States of America

Library of Congress Cataloging-in-Publication Data

Thomas, Emory M., 1939–
  Travels to hallowed ground.

  (American military history)
  1. United States—History—Civil War, 1861–1865—
Battlefields.   2. United States—History—Civil War,
1861–1865—Campaigns.   3. Thomas, Emory M.,
1939–   —Journeys—United States.   I. Title.
II. Series: American military history (Columbia, S.C.)
E641.T47   1987   973.7   86-30782
ISBN 0-87249-477-2
ISBN 0-87249-498-5 (pbk.)

To
Mary Morton Thomas and W. Lynn Thomas

CONTENTS

ILLUSTRATIONS

MAPS

ACKNOWLEDGMENTS

The author wishes to thank the editor of *Civil War Times Illustrated* for permission to use portions of materials originally published therein in May 1976 (herein "Roanoke Island and Murphy's Law"), in April 1977 (herein "Torpedoes and Time on Mobile Bay"), and in February, April 1978 (herein "Total War and Apricot Jam").

The author gratefully acknowledges the permission of Harper & Row, Publishers, Inc. to quote material from his *Bold Dragoon: The Life of J.E.B. Stuart*, Harper & Row, 1986 (herein "Riding with a Calculating Cavalier").

Travels to Hallowed Ground

HISTORY AND HALLOWED GROUND:

An Introduction

Abraham Lincoln went to Gettysburg (in November of 1863) and said, among other things, "We can not consecrate—we cannot hallow—this ground. The brave men, living and dead, who struggled here, have consecrated it, far above our poor power to add or detract."

I went to Gettysburg in May of 1985 and discovered that we have certainly tried to consecrate this ground. An average of one million of us make pilgrimages to Gettysburg every year to see the shrine. As a result these sacred acres have endured an absolutely harrowing degree of hallowing.

There is a reason for all this—the same reason that brought Lincoln to Gettysburg to say that we could not make this place any more sacred. Somewhere, amid the Lincoln Train Museum, the National Civil War Wax Museum, the Hall of Presidents and First Ladies, the Home Sweet Home Motel, the National Tower, and the Get-Mor Factory Outlet, 150,000 men fought a horrendous battle here. After three terrible days, nearly one-third of these men were dead, wounded, or prisoners. In this place the fate of the United States and the Confederate States hung in suspense; when the fighting subsided, many of the survivors believed that something important had occurred. And the hindsight of history and historians has tended to confirm this judgment.

Robert E. Lee came to Pennsylvania to fight a climactic battle, and the Federal Army of the Potomac followed, as Lee knew it would.

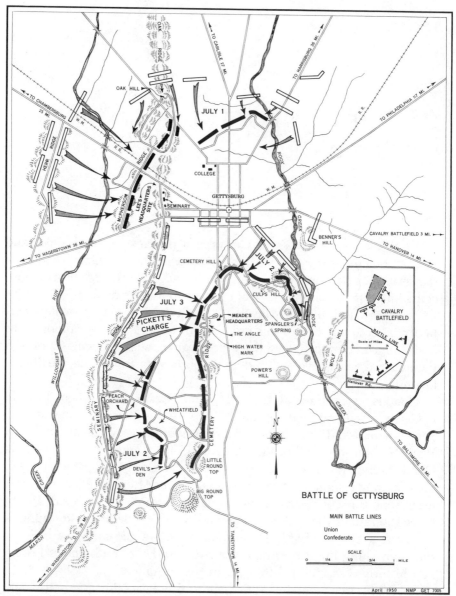

The Battle of Gettysburg.

George G. Meade became commander of the Union force on June 28, 1863, and soon after marched his men north to contest the Confederates who were scattered over south-central Pennsylvania living off the country. The armies collided at Gettysburg on July 1.

On that first day of the great battle, one of the initial factors was shoes. The Confederates believed that at Gettysburg was a supply of shoes, and the Southerners determined to have them. At this point the Confederates did not know that the growing numbers of Federal soldiers who contested the town were the leading elements of Meade's army. They did not know this because J.E.B. Stuart and his cavalry, Lee's "eyes," were still on a protracted raid, actually riding away from Gettysburg, in effect, and in fact lost to Lee's army.

The fight for Gettysburg on July 1 gradually grew in intensity and became Richard S. Ewell's battle. Ewell commanded one of Lee's corps, Stonewall Jackson's men for the most part, and during the late afternoon the Southerners swept into Gettysburg. But there Ewell stopped, while his enemies held the higher ground (Cemetery and Culp's hills) south of the town. Lee had ordered this ground taken "if possible"; but as the daylight waned, Ewell decided that it was not possible and cited the authority of another of Lee's instructions, not to risk a general engagement before the Southern army had concentrated.

Troop units from both armies continued to reach the scene during the night and next day (July 2). Meade arrived and decided to make a stand in this place. More precisely Meade arrayed his men on the elevated ground due south of the town—from Cemetery and Culp's hills down Cemetery Ridge eventually to the steeper heights of Little Round Top and Big Round Top. Lee's army concentrated across the Emmitsburg Road to the west on Seminary Ridge.

Lee determined to attack on July 2, before the Union army consolidated. He ordered James Longstreet's corps to strike the Federal left flank in front of the Round Tops and Ewell to assault the Federal right around Culp's Hill. Longstreet was late (4:00 P.M.) and Ewell later still. In furious fighting the Federals held their high ground, but just barely.

At dark the Confederates formed an ominous "fishhook" around the critical terrain—from the eastern base of Culp's Hill, around Cemetery Hill, down the gentler slope of Cemetery Ridge, into the glacial tailing of Devil's Den at the base of Little Round Top, and to the western slope of Big Round Top.

During the night Meade gathered his principal subordinates and asked them whether he should stay in place or withdraw. His corps commanders urged Meade to remain and fight, and he did.

Longstreet urged Lee to abandon this ground and move around the Federal left, between Meade's army and Washington. Such a shift, he believed, would compel Meade to attack Lee, and perhaps Longstreet envisioned another Fredericksburg in which the Federals battered themselves to pieces in futile assaults. But Lee sought success on the offense, not the defense, and maybe remembered Chancellorsville where he had come so close to destroying his enemy. He determined to attack. He had assaulted the Federal flanks; now he would attack the very center of the Union army and break the Federal battle line. Confederate infantry would strike Cemetery Ridge; Stuart's cavalry, finally arrived, would strike the Federal rear.

So on July 3 at 1:00 P.M. Confederate artillery, 159 guns, began firing at Cemetery Ridge and continued firing for more than an hour until their ammunition was all but gone. Federal guns responded, but ceased after an hour, encouraging Southerners to believe that they had exhausted their ammunition or that they were casualties of the Confederate barrage.

Then George Pickett's fresh division led 12,000 Southern men from the woods. The Confederates formed as though on parade and poured toward the Union line on Cemetery Ridge. Federal artillery opened a devastating fire and Federal foot soldiers attacked the flanks. From his vantage point on Seminary Ridge, Lee could see that Pickett's charge was doomed. Some of the Southerners made it into the Federal lines; most of those who did never returned. The charge was a gallant disaster.

Meanwhile Stuart's horsemen suffered a similar fate about two and a

half miles away. Stuart launched his cavalry pell mell against his enemies; but the Federals broke up the assault and Stuart never came close
to supporting the infantry attack.

In the wake of Pickett's Charge, Lee was frank to admit his failure.
"It's all my fault," he said, and he was right. Subsequently, generations
of professional and amateur analysts have blamed Ewell for halting
short of the crucial hills on the first day and Stuart for leaving Lee
"blind" to the location and strength of Meade's oncoming army. They
have blamed Longstreet for his late and somewhat uncoordinated attacks on the second day and for dispatching Pickett when Southern artillery could no longer support him on the third day. But the responsibility
was Lee's, and he assumed it. And still tourists and experts wonder why
Lee chose to attack and to attack the Federal center on July 3.

William Faulkner may have come closest to saying why Lee did what
he did. Faulkner wrote it in *Intruder in the Dust* when he wrote:

It's all *now* you see. Yesterday wont be over until tomorrow and tomorrow began ten thousand years ago. For every Southern boy
fourteen years old, not once but whenever he wants it, there is the
instant when it's still not yet two o'clock on that July afternoon in
1863, the brigades are in position behind the rail fence, the guns are
laid and ready in the woods and the furled flags are already loos-
ened to break out and Pickett himself with his long oiled ringlets
and his hat in one hand probably and his sword in the other looking up the hill waiting for Longstreet to give the word and it's all in
the balance, it hasn't happened yet, it hasn't even begun yet, it not
only hasn't begun yet but there is still time for it not to begin
against that position and those circumstances which made more
men than Garnett and Kemper and Armstead [*sic*] and Wilcox
look grave yet it's going to begin, we all know that, we have come
too far with too much at stake and that moment doesn't need even
a fourteen-year-old boy to think *This time. Maybe this time* with
all this much to lose and all this much to gain: Pennsylvania, Mary-

Matthew Brady's photograph of Gettysburg as it appeared from Seminary Ridge shortly after the battle. Courtesy of the National Park Service.

land, the world, the golden dome of Washington itself to crown with desperate and unbelievable victory the gamble, the case made two years ago; or to anyone who ever sailed even a skiff under a quilt sail, the moment in 1492 when somebody thought *This is it;* the absolute edge of no return, to turn back now and make home or sail irrevocably on and either find land or plunge over the world's roaring rim.

Lee faced what he perceived as the moment of truth and refused to flinch. His enemy, "those people" as he called them, were over there. He

David Muench's photograph [©David Muench 1987] of Seminary Ridge and the town of Gettysburg as they are today.

had come too far, risked too much, to shrink from this opportunity to strike them.

Gettysburg is a vast terrain well-marked. Because and in spite of the banalities of tourism, there is a transcendence at Gettysburg between past and present. On Cemetery Ridge a small grove of hardwood trees was and is the Confederate "High Water Mark."

Soldiers who made Pickett's Charge used these trees as a guide and goal. Some of them reached a low stone wall just in front of the trees and there encountered the primary Federal infantry line. The Southerners had exposed themselves to vicious artillery and small-arms fire. Nevertheless, survivors filled gaps left by their fallen comrades, snatched up their colors when they fell, and swept forward. At the stone wall, however, the attackers hesitated. And then Lewis Armistead, the only Confederate general still with the men, placed his hat on the tip of his sword and held it aloft. "Boys, give them cold steel!" he screamed and clambered over the wall. Men followed Armistead over the wall and into the Union lines. But there they suffered more murderous fire from Federal reinforcements. Armistead fell mortally wounded. They were suddenly so few amid so many of their enemies. And finally those who were able turned and fled, back over the low wall, down the gentle slope.

Now all around the small grove on Cemetery Ridge are cannon and monuments and a bronze book which lists the units that fought here. I imagined Armistead with his hat still on his sword and contemplated the chaos of that July afternoon in this place.

Cars rolled slowly along Hancock Avenue; guides told stories and pointed out landmarks; couples and families inspected the ground and gazed in all directions. Then a school bus from the Holy Name of Jesus School unleashed its cargo of boys and girls (sixth graders?) along with some weary-looking adults. They had a guide with them, and he was earning every penny of his fee this day. The youngsters were milling about laughing and talking and periodically darting from one small group of themselves to another. The guide was about to introduce these young Americans to the role of artillery in the Civil War. "I need six volunteers," he called out. The general din subsided and a forest of raised hands appeared. Carefully the guide selected six of the hands. Then he told them that they were going to play the horses which pulled the field piece. Everyone laughed. The boys and girls continued to climb on the cannon and enjoy the warm, spring day.

Past and present were intersecting here at the Confederate high water mark. On the hallowed ground of Gettysburg, Clio, the ancient Greek muse of history, was face to face with a bus load of expectant sixth graders. What would this place mean to those boys and girls? Would they incorporate the experience of those 150,000 soldiers so long ago into their experience in the late twentieth century? What *does* Gettysburg mean? Once more "it is all in the balance."

This is a book of stories and thoughts provoked by my own confrontation with hallowed ground, trips to places where history happened. I visited some of the many sites associated with the American Civil War. I went to places as well-known as Bull Run, Harpers Ferry and Shiloh; I visited some pretty obscure spots, too, such as the intersection of Virginia routes 14 and 620 where Ulric Dahlgren tumbled from his horse with five bullets in his body.

I have tried to tell interesting stories as vividly as I can. I have attempted to offer reflections, profound and profane, about these stories and about past and place. My commentary is often irreverent. I hope that my collection of travels and tales is, at the same time, thought-provoking and entertaining.

RIGHT AND RIGHTEOUSNESS AT HARPERS FERRY

Harpers Ferry is a beautiful place in "wild and wonderful" West Virginia. There the Shenandoah River joins the Potomac, and mountains slope down to the flowing waters. Early on a spring morning when I arrived, the mist was still rising from the rivers, and the view from almost anywhere was gorgeous—"stupendous" was Thomas Jefferson's adjective in 1783.

The Harpers Ferry National Historical Park dominates this triangle of land between the rivers. The park features people in period costumes and restored or preserved buildings; the place is well on the way to becoming a nineteenth-century Williamsburg. Also within the park are trails to hike, rocks to climb, and industrial ruins to explore. But my primary attraction to Harpers Ferry (and I suspect that of most visitors) was not the scenery, the restorations, trails, rocks, or ruins. I went to Harpers Ferry because of John Brown.

Brown was an enigmatic man who achieved both fame and infamy at Harpers Ferry. On the evening of October 16, 1859, he led a force of twenty-two men, his "army of liberation," into this town of three thousand people. Brown intended to seize control of Harpers Ferry and its arsenal to establish a base from which to strike a blow against slavery. Convinced that runaway slaves would flock to his banner, Brown hoped to begin in this place a massive emancipation of Southern slaves. After some initial success, however, his poorly made plans went awry. By the evening of October 17, Brown and six of his followers had barricaded themselves in a brick fire engine house with thirteen prisoners. Next morning (October 18) a detachment of United States Marines commanded by Robert E. Lee stormed the fire engine house, quashed the abortive coup, and captured Brown.

Six weeks later (December 2) in Charles Town, Brown was hanged for murder, treason, and conspiring to generate a slave insurrection. The day he died, he wrote, "I, John Brown, am now quite certain that the crimes of this guilty land will never be purged away but with blood." Perhaps as he had planned, certainly as he predicted, the American Civil War fulfilled Brown's final prophecy.

I wandered about the restored town for a while thinking about John Brown and his raid. Then I went to see the film that introduces park visitors to Brown's story and the events of October, 1859.

Black actor, director, and playwright Ossie Davis narrated Brown's story and offered a summary of slavery as Southern institution and sectional issue. Verbally and visually Davis made the point that Harpers Ferry compelled and still compels Americans to confront slavery as a moral issue. Harpers Ferry also compelled and still compels Americans to confront the merits of extralegal (in this case, violent) action as a response to injustice.

To underscore these points the film used clips from "sidewalk seminars" in which visitors and tourists shared a wide range of reactions to Brown and his attempted coup. One person insisted that in the context of the times slaves were property, and thus Brown was a thief. Another considered Brown justified in striking any blow against so heinous a system as slavery. Many applauded Brown's motives, but questioned his means.

Ossie Davis's narration, his use of quotations from Brown, Jefferson Davis, and others, the blend of images, photographs and drawings of the period combined with present-time pictures of the restored setting, and the responses of modern Americans were still rolling through my head as I shuffled toward the exit. I left the auditorium thinking that this was one of the very best history films I had ever seen. It told the story and informed the viewer; it also challenged the viewer to ask the important questions about Brown and Harpers Ferry. But the film, like history, did not provide precise or prescribed answers to those questions. Like history, the film inspired people to think.

I was walking behind a middle-aged couple. As we reached the street, the man asked the woman what she thought of the film. "It was all right," she said, "but I thought it would have more history in it."

Inside the reconstructed fire engine house I returned to the events of October in 1859. I thought some more about the life and death of John Brown.

Standing in this place where Brown had been at bay, it was tempting to press him into the context of civil disobedience and so link him with people like Henry David Thoreau, Mohandas Gandhi, Martin Luther King, Jr., and Desmond Tutu. Brown, however, does not belong in that tradition. His goal was freedom; his cause was just. But his means were mean. In 1856 Brown had directed the cold-blooded "executions" of five proslavery settlers on Pottawatomie Creek in Kansas. At Harpers Ferry the first man to die in Brown's attack was Hayward Shepherd, a free black man who was baggagemaster at the railway station. Brown was a rigid Calvinist who allowed hate, rather than love, to define and ultimately consume him. Murder and martyrdom do not mix.

Here in his "fort" on October 17, Brown was not yet the aspiring martyr he later became. I was impressed with how very small the fire engine house was, no larger than lots of suburban living rooms. And crowded inside for quite some time were twenty men (Brown, six of his men, and thirteen prisoners). At this point the prisoners became hostages. Brown offered their lives in exchange for freedom for himself and his remaining men. Although armed citizens and militia units surrounded the engine house and two of Brown's men (his sons) were dying from wounds, the old man still controlled the fate of his hostages. Into this impasse came Lee and his marines, sent from Washington to quell the disturbance.

Amid the issues involving Brown and his actions here, it is too easy to overlook Lee's role in the drama. The situation was indeed tense, and

the story of Brown's capture and the release of his hostages deserves re-
telling.

Lee quickly took charge of the situation. First he assured himself that
the engine house was securely surrounded; then he surveyed the ground
and made his plans. Soon after midnight on the eighteenth Lee wrote
out a message to Brown. In the note Lee identified himself and demanded surrender. Pointing out "in all frankness" that escape was impossible, Lee stated that if he were "compelled to take them by force," he
could not "answer for their safety." He gave the message to a young lieutenant who had accompanied him from Washington, J.E.B. Stuart,
with instructions about when and how to deliver it.

Lee ordered Stuart approach the engine house door under a white
flag of truce and pass his message inside. In the likely event that Brown
refused to surrender, Stuart was to refuse to bargain. As soon as he determined that Brown had understood and rejected the demand, Stuart
was supposed to give a signal. Then a storming party standing by would
rush the engine house.

Early on the morning of October 18 Lee prepared the storming party.
First the commander of the Maryland militia units and then the Virginia militia commander declined the duty on behalf of their men. Both
suggested that professional, instead of part-time, soldiers should under-
take the risks involved. Accordingly, Lee asked Lieutenant Israel Greene
if he and his marines would perform the task. Greene then chose twelve
of his men and instructed them to fix bayonets. Lee permitted no loaded
weapons for fear of harming the hostages.

At seven o'clock in the morning all was ready. With about 2000
people—soldiers and civilians—watching, Stuart stepped into the open
and walked to the door of the engine house carrying his white flag. John
Brown, himself, opened the door a crack and pushed a carbine in Stuart's face.

Brown listened while Stuart read the demand for his surrender; then
at once he tried to bargain. No sooner had Stuart informed him that Lee
wanted an immediate, yes-or-no response, than Brown posed another

An old photograph of the entrance to the U.S. Armory grounds at Harpers Ferry, the fire engine house at the left, the machine shops where the muskets were assembled at the right. Courtesy of the National Park Service.

The restored engine house.

compromise. Some of the hostages added their voices urging Stuart to soften the terms. But one of the hostages, Lewis W. Washington, who was George Washington's grandnephew and whom Lee knew well, shouted, "Never mind us, fire." Lee heard this and reflected out loud, "The old revolutionary blood does tell."

After some time, Stuart realized that Brown did not intend to surrender. He stepped back from the door and waved his hat as a signal to Greene and his marines.

Three of them ran to the door and began to pound it with sledgehammers. The blows had little effect, and the defenders began shooting at the storming party. Then Greene ordered his men to drop their hammers and use a ladder as a battering ram. The second thrust opened a small hole in the door, and Greene led his men inside.

Two marines were shot as they entered, but the rest made short work of the defenders. They bayoneted to death two of Brown's men; two more surrendered. Greene himself attacked Brown with a light sword. Before Brown could fire his cocked weapon, Greene hit him with his sword, then tried to run him through, and finally pummeled him about the head until Brown was unconscious.

From the time Stuart waved his hat the entire action took only a few minutes. No harm came to any of the hostages. Lee had made the best of a very volatile circumstance.

Harpers Ferry is still John Brown's place. The issues and questions Brown raised here by his deeds continue to be important in American life. But in times marked by hijacking, hostages, and terror, Lee's actions, too, deserve recalling. Brown's soul still marches on in that corporate memory which is history. He attempted to act out righteousness, and his actions still challenge Americans to confront racism and response to racial and other wrongs. But Lee, too, acted here. And his actions speak to decisive leadership.

BULL RUN OUTSIDE
THE SANDBOX

It all began in a sandbox. When I teach a college course on the American Civil War, I use the First Battle of Bull Run to conclude a presentation entitled "Eve of Destruction" on the nature of warfare in the 1860s. The battle serves as a case study in combat at this early stage of the war. After sketching maps on the blackboard and showing slides of photographs taken on the battlefield, I do a crude reenactment of the conflict in a four- by eight-foot sandbox, using small plastic soldiers. The sandbox demonstration permits students to view critical stages of the battle in three dimensions, and thus they understand better how and why events took place as they did. College students seem to enjoy playing in the sand, and I suspect Maria Montessori would have approved.

By the time the students have read, heard, and reenacted the Battle of First Manassas, they pretty well know the essential facts of July 21, 1861. On that day a Union army of approximately 35,000 men commanded by Irwin McDowell encountered a Confederate force of equal numbers led by P. G. T. Beauregard. The Southerners were drawn up along the south bank of Bull Run; Beauregard's strength included some 15,000 troops recently arrived from the Shenandoah Valley, and with this concentration he meant to attack. The Federals struck the first blow, however, as McDowell launched an assault across the stone bridge on the left of the Confederate battle line. More Federals crossed Bull Run at Sudley Springs Ford, beyond the Confederate left flank and threatened to roll up the Southern line. The Confederates made a stand on Henry House

Hill, and there Thomas Jonathan Jackson earned his nickname "Stonewall" for his steadfastness. The battle raged for hours across the slopes of Henry House Hill as units from each army in turn joined the fight and attempted to outflank the Confederate left or Union right.

Finally at about four o'clock in the afternoon Beauregard, who was on the scene, saw still more troops approaching the field from the west. Fearing the worst, he prepared to retreat in order to save his army from complete destruction. Then, at all but the last moment, Beauregard was able to see the flag at the head of the advancing column—it was a Confederate flag. As the fresh brigade neared the Federal flank, the entire Southern line began a spontaneous charge. The first recorded "rebel yell" shrieked above the sounds of battle. The Union line wavered, then broke, as McDowell's soldiers withdrew across Bull Run. Retreat turned to rout as weary, frightened men sought safety and clogged the roads leading back toward Washington. Beauregard's Confederates were tired, disorganized, and only slightly less afraid than their fleeing foes. Thus the Southerners were unable to follow up their victory, and the battle wound down.

For perhaps a dozen years I had taught college students about the battle without ever having seen the scene. Surely it was time to go to the ground I had known only from maps and photographs, to see the terrain I had so many times sculpted in sand, and to seek whatever historical transcendence was in that place.

To get to Manassas from most places it is necessary to travel Interstate Route 95 and then a state route that winds through an area in transition. A few dairy barns, some fenced pastures, and scattered stands of hardwood trees offer evidence of what the countryside must have all been like twenty years ago. New subdivisions with names like Camelot and Clover Hill and Seven-Eleven convenience stores at cross-roads bear witness to the spread of Washington's bedrooms and presage the growing megalopolis of the eastern seaboard. And between the scenery of past and future is an ugly present, marked by an obsession with automobiles. The houses are small and shabby so that the automobiles can be large and several, and I suppose people must have the automobiles (and spend their weekends working on them) so they can drive distances to work. Whatever the reason, there are sad little houses in clusters along the roadside, surrounded by automobiles in various states of repair, and some fenced fields, which probably once contained cows, now harbor rows of rusting cars.

Manassas still has railroad tracks to recall the time the village was Manassas Junction and to recall one of the reasons Beauregard chose to make his stand here. The Confederate reinforcements from the Shenandoah Valley, as well as war supplies, and even Jefferson Davis the Confederate President reached Manassas by "the cars" as the expression for rail travel was then.

Across the tracks in the center of town is a business district that for the most part looked to me circa 1965. Surrounding this center were neighborhoods with homes that ranged from stately to quaint, most of them in various stages of renovation. Beyond this core were shopping centers, a mall, subdivisions, apartment complexes, and condominiums. This is "NoVa," northern Virginia, a bland blend of crowded convenience, the American roots of which an architectural genealogist would probably find in Levittown.

Amid the predictable facades of American life in the late twentieth century, the Manassas commercial community does acknowledge the locality's primary claim to fame, the event that occurred in the mid-nineteenth century. In honor of the battle or the stream there are Bull Run Cycles, Bull Run Kennels, the Bull Run Mobile Home Park, Bull Run Stone Company, Bull Run Valve Company, and more. There is a "Battlefield" Ford, and Exxon, Builders, Insurance Agency, Realty, Shell, Sunoco, Supply Company, and Texaco. And to commemorate that stern Calvinist who acquired his sobriquet nearby is the Stonewall Lounge at the Holiday House restaurant.

Beyond the "condo curtain" surrounding Manassas, across Interstate 66, is the battlefield park. A split-rail fence encloses rolling acres, fields and woods forming an uncluttered oasis amid suburban sprawl. Surely

The Stone Bridge, photographed in 1862. Courtesy of the National Archives and *Civil War Times Illustrated*.

it is ironic that the most peaceful place in the neighborhood is a battle-field.

Actually the battlefield park had recently been the subject of a verbal and legislative conflict known as the "Third Battle of Manassas" shortly before my visit. In 1940 when Washington was still far away and

The Stone Bridge today. Courtesy of Manassas National Battlefield Park and *Civil War Times Illustrated.*

"NoVa" was a term used almost exclusively by astronomers, the United States Congress created the park and endowed it with about 1700 acres. Forty years later Congress added just under 1400 acres, but only after a long and sometimes bitter battle that began in 1976 between battlefields buffs and "the developers." Now the park contains precisely 3,031.67

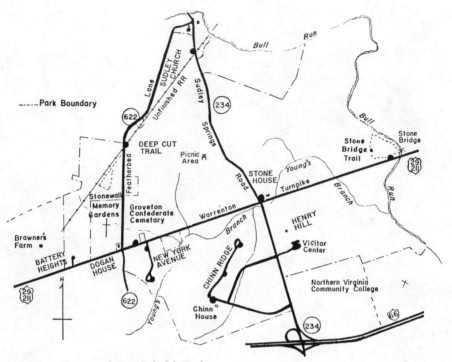

Manassas National Battlefield Park.

acres, and the preservationists claim a narrow victory. The park itself bears no scars of Third Manassas which took place in committee rooms, letters, newsletters, and newspapers far away.

I went first to the Visitor Center which is an imposing columned building near Henry House Hill. There I picked up a leaflet describing the battles and watched a slide-tape presentation. Also in the Visitor Center was a molded three-dimensional map of the terrain upon which a programmed series of colored lights shone to portray the tactical story of the two battles. I was impressed, but came away wondering if the National Park Service would be interested in my sandbox and little soldiers. Colored lights just do not look like people. I was reminded of some lines about Manassas in Stephen Vincent Benét's *John Brown's Body:*

> If you take a flat map
> And move wooden blocks upon it strategically
> The thing looks well, the blocks behave as they should.

But at Manassas, as Benét knew, the soldiers were "still used to just being men, not block parts." Maybe the ground would have meaning; after all I had not come here to see the sorts of things I could do in a classroom.

The taped narration of the battles employed the phrase "plains of Manassas," and it is accurate. The ground was mostly open and cleared in 1861; indeed the Park Service was at work cutting down cedar trees to maintain the vegetation level approximately as it had been. This land gives meaning to the word "undulate" and distances can be deceiving in the rolling country. December is not exactly the height of the visitor season in northern Virginia, and I had the place pretty much to myself. Each year an average of about 800,000 people come to Manassas; but when I was there, my fellow travelers were few.

There were almost as many runners as tourists. They were definitely runners, as opposed to joggers; they were lean, and some were glancing at watches. Lean people who run with watches in December are usually serious about the activity. The young men who marched here in 1861 had not trained for this for very long, and they were here in July when it was hot. They wore wool uniforms, carried knapsacks and blanket rolls, and hefted heavy rifles as they marched. The lives they lived in peacetime were more physically demanding than ours, and so they were probably more physically fit than most modern Americans. People who had to split stove wood in order to eat breakfast may not have needed to do all that many sets of reverse curls; and before internal combustion engines, people were likely to have been in better aerobic condition. Nevertheless, the men who fought here must have suffered from the exertion; the Federals had to march many miles just to reach these plains, and most of the Confederates had marched just as far on the day of the battle. Add fear and confusion to these physical demands, and I wonder at the stamina of those men.

I recalled Curly Hatton. He is a fictional Confederate in *John Brown's Body*, and Benét used him to display, among other things, the physical demands of being a soldier here. Curly is fat—"Butterball-legs under a butterball-body"—and he despises the road—"Because there was so much of it ahead / And all of it so dry." Curly is in love and diverts his mind from his aching feet with fantasies of cool evenings with his fair Lucy. Benét brings Curly Hatton back periodically as his account of First Manassas unfolds. Curly goes into action near the crest of Henry House Hill—"His butterball-legs moved faster—Lucy—Lucy—" Later after the conflict has raged about the hill for some time, "Curly Hatton was nothing any more / But a dry throat and a pair of burnt black hands / That held a hot gun he was always firing." Then he is annoyed by a noise when he must fall down and vomit. It is "The dolefully nasty noise of a badly-hurt dog." And he realizes that it is he making the noise and he cannot stop. Finally Curly Hatton awakens in a darkened church that shelters wounded men. He watches Lucy's face dissolve in his mind's eye and knows he will die.

From the pages of a diary found on this field after the battle emerges a character more engaging than the fictional Curly Hatton. His name was G. T. Anderson. He fought here, and he was real. He enlisted in the Fourth Alabama Regiment in Huntsville, and on April 29 Anderson boarded a boxcar with other members of his regiment, including his brother Stephen, bound for northern Virginia. En route he wrote in his diary on May 4, "Woke up in Jonesboro, Tenn., about sunrise; saw lots of beautiful women; received a bouquet from a very nice girl with a soul-stirring inscription on it." Anderson rode and marched all the way to Harper's Ferry. He had "to make out for two days on bread and meat that a dog would refuse." He was homesick: "Why on earth can't a fellow hear from home? They seem to have forgotten that we are in the world. I have a notion not to write any more until I receive a letter from home." He complained that his colonel was an "aristocrat—dog him." Then finally on May 18, "The long-looked for letter comes at last, and O how much joy it gives us; all well at home, though we feared otherwise, and all miss us and want to see us, but no worse than we want to see them. We are satisfied now." Anderson and his brother cried over the letter.

On May 19 the Fourth Alabama was inspected by "Colonel Jackson" who would shortly be "Stonewall" Jackson. Anderson was not impressed, "He is a large fat old fellow; looks very much like an old Virginia farmer."

On May 22 Anderson reflected:

Three trains of troops have just arrived. I look for hot work soon. Troops are coming in here every day and surely they are not coming here just to be coming. We may look for a fight within three weeks, and if I fall I hope that God will pardon my sins. I want to pray and be saved, but I am too much of a sinner—I fear that I never will. It is horrible to think of dying, leaving a world of sorrow and going straight to a worse. From such a fate, O God, in mercy, save me.

Both Anderson and his brother were sick in late May–early June. They recovered in time to fall back with the regiment to Winchester on June 14, and Anderson confessed a wish "to see some of the ladies of Winchester—the best kind."

Then on July 18, he "received orders to strike tents and cook two days' provisions preparatory for a march. This was done and we lay around until evening before receiving orders." When those orders arrived, the Fourth Alabama marched all night, slept two hours, marched to the Shenandoah River, rested about five hours there, and then resumed the march. Anderson covered nearly twenty-five miles in less than thirty hours, and: "Arrived at Piedmont station about one hour after dark, completely worn out. Went to sleep, but was aroused by rain in a few minutes. Crept under a shelter of wheat, but got wet, having left my coat in the wagon. Dried myself, procured a shawl from Uncle Washington [the regimental quartermaster] and slept until midnight."

At that time, the earliest hours of July 20 the Fourth Alabama boarded the train for Manassas. Anderson arrived around 10:00 A.M., rested a short time, then marched two miles, and camped near the home of Wilmer McLean. When some bread and meat reached the men, they "walked right into it like starved hounds eat, now and then all day."

Next morning, July 21, the day of the battle Anderson, "Got up a little after sunrise. . . broiled my meat and ate it with some old crackers full of bugs. Expecting order to march every moment. . . . We shall fight, I suppose, before another week."

Anderson closed his diary after writing those words and did get orders to march before 7:00 A.M. The Fourth Alabama, with the second Mississippi and two companies of the Eleventh Mississippi, followed General Bernard E. Bee toward the stone bridge where the Warrenton Pike (now Routes 29 and 211) crossed Bull Run. Bee's undersized brigade marched at the double-quick for four miles; then Bee learned of the Union threat from the left down the Manassas—Sudley Road (now Route 234), Bee changed direction and double-quick marched over Henry House Hill through the corn fields to the beleaguered battle line of Colonel Nathan "Shanks" Evans. The Confederates of Evans' command first felt the weight of the primary Federal advance from Sudley Springs Ford. When Anderson and his comrades reached the scene, some oak woods on the slope of Matthews Hill, at about 10:00 A.M., the rapid marching had taken a toll, and an Alabama captain termed their condition "much exhausted." The Southerners lay on the ground only about a hundred yards from their enemies and began firing.

Artillery batteries augmented the fire of Federal infantry, and in this critical front the Federals outnumbered the Confederates better than two to one. When the artillery found the range, the Southerners charged.

The Fourth Alabama moved through a cornfield and then up a slight

rise into the face of the Federal batteries. The Alabamians advanced far-
ther and held their ground longer than did any other unit involved. But
after an hour or more they had to fall back toward the Warrenton Turnpike and Henry House Hill. G. T. Anderson did not accompany his regiment in the retreat. During the assault upon the Second Rhode Island
Artillery, a grapeshot struck him in the cheek. He died instantly.

The remnants of the Fourth Alabama Regiment withdrew from the
field where G. T. Anderson fell, back over Matthews Hill, across the
Warrenton Pike, and up the slope of Henry House Hill. Those men of
General Bee's command who remained were much confused. Many of
the missing were officers, and the leaderless soldiers milled about in
search of friends and order. Bee did not even recognize the Fourth Alabama when he saw no one in the unit whom he knew. The harassed
commander did find a brigade in good order on top of Henry House
Hill; its commander was Thomas J. Jackson, G. T. Anderson's "large fat
old fellow." Jackson had artillery in place and firing; but his infantry
troops were simply lying down just back of the crest of the hill.

Bee exclaimed to Jackson, "General, they are beating us back."

"Sir, we'll give them the bayonet," was Jackson's response.

Then Bee rode off to rejoin what was left of his command. He must
have interpreted Jackson's statement as an order to attack, because he
formed his men and led them forward into the advancing Federals.

But before he did so, Bee exhorted the troops. One account of what he
said was, "There is Jackson standing like a stone wall. Let us determine
to die here, and we will conquer. Follow me." Another version was,
"Look at Jackson's brigade; it stands like a stone wall! Rally behind the
Virginians." Whatever the wording, Bee likened Jackson and his command to a stone wall, and the simile stuck. But what did Bee mean? I
would like to believe that he referred to Jackson's steadfast determina-
tion to hold this ground in the face of adversity. Under the circumstances, though, quite another interpretation is possible, even probable.
Bee may have meant to hold Jackson up to ridicule and criticism for being a "stone wall," unwilling or unable to move or fight. In this context

Bee was saying words to the effect, "Jackson will not attack, so we will have to save the day."

Whatever Bee did say or mean to say, he was soon unavailable to repeat or explain. He launched his assault and led his men into battle. But quickly the advance faltered in the face of withering fire, and Bee suffered a mortal wound. He died some hours later, and Thomas Jonathan Jackson's nickname has been his most enduring legacy.

Standing on Henry House Hill where Jackson's troops had lain that day, I was impressed with the relatively confined area in which so much had happened. I realized that the rolling terrain foreshortened the distances; yet thousands of men had confronted each other and the battle had raged for hours just within my glance. There were markers at each of several critical points on the hill with recorded messages, told as though the voices were those of participants, and I could see each of these stations and the entire circuit of markers was less than a mile. It seemed Fates, Furies, or whatever had defined and confined the battlefield and two large armies had come here, almost as athletic teams travel to stadia and playing fields, to do mortal combat. There were even spectators that day in 1861. People had packed lunches and driven in their carriages from Washington to watch the battle. They could sit or stand on those hills just north of Bull Run and see the action as though they were watching a sports event. But this was no game and all analogies that link war to athletic contests are dangerous. Men died here. And those who survived did not shuffle off to locker rooms, take showers, and then meet wives or girl friends; they remained in the heat and dirt to bury their friends. In a larger sense, too, the "game" analogy to war fails. The stakes were very high here, and because they were, winners could impose their will upon losers. What happened here involved considerably more than "bragging rights."

Maybe the absence of trenches, breastworks, or field fortifications produced the illusion of this battlefield as playing field. As the war progressed, soldiers would learn the folly of trying to survive on open ground. They scooped up soil with any implement they could find in search of greater safety. Here the soldiers had not yet learned that lesson, and the battle was fluid; so the land was unscarred here.

However neat and confined Henry House Hill seemed to me, the total battlefield was extensive and the armies that occupied this land were larger than any yet known in North America. There had been larger armies in Europe, of course, and there would be much larger armies later in this war. But at this point no one on either side had ever tried to command so many men in combat. Thus it was small wonder that the battle simply seemed to happen, to generate some inner dynamic that defied the efforts of the generals to control the day.

Generals Beauregard and Johnston had tried to conduct the battle from a headquarters. Beauregard had dispatched complicated orders that were never implemented, while the sounds of guns grew louder from the west. When Douglas S. Freeman wrote about First Manassas in *Lee's Lieutenants*, he used double columns on these pages. One column explained what was going on at various times during the morning; the second column related what Beauregard and Johnston believed was happening. Rarely did the two accounts coincide. Finally Johnston, who outranked Beauregard but had let him plan the battle, could stand the suspense and confusion no longer. "The battle is there," he said referring to the Confederate left flank, "I am going." Johnston mounted his horse, Beauregard followed, and the two commanders rode off to find out what was happening to their command.

The two generals arrived at Henry House Hill in the wake of Bee's aborted charge. Both men waded into the chaos and attempted to restore order among the survivors. At this point, it seemed to me, the generals made their most significant direct contribution to the battle. Beauregard's written orders had had no effect; the only worthwhile command the Confederates had given was the simple, oral directive, "Go to the sound of the firing." And now the generals were appointing officers and getting soldiers back into line.

Meanwhile McDowell was confident of victory. He had had the better plan, and so far, it was working. Yet many of his troops were still marching toward the field, instead of pressing the attack, and McDowell's most important order was words to the effect "Hurry up!"

Following a brief lull around noon, the battle raged across Henry House Hill for most of the afternoon. By this time, however, the Henry House of Henry House Hill was in shambles. The modest frame structure has been rebuilt and it stands in a small grove of trees near the crest of the hill. Nearby is a family graveyard, and in one of the graves is Judith Carter Henry who died on July 21, 1861, from wounds suffered in this battle.

At the Henry House that morning were an 85-year-old bedridden widow, Mrs. Henry, her son, her daughter, and a hired black woman. When the battle began to come near, Mrs. Henry's son and daughter made plans to move her to a safer place. But things happened in a hurry, and the best they could do was to get themselves and the old woman to a springhouse nearby. And there Mrs. Henry demanded that she be returned to her bed. The three younger members of the household complied with her wishes. No sooner had they done so, than the same Rhode Island Artillery which had fired the grape-sized ball of lead into G. T. Anderson's face opened fire on the Henry House. The commander believed that Confederate sharpshooters were firing from within; so "I turned my guns upon the house and literally riddled it."

John Henry, the son, was outside when the barrage began; daughter Ellen crawled inside the fireplace; and the black woman lay under Mrs. Henry's bed. A shot soon plowed through the frame wall and hit the bed. Judith Henry was knocked out of bed and wounded mortally. As she died she tried to reassure her frantic daughter.

I imagined the horror and terror in the Henry household on that day when war visited their front yard. These people should not have been there; but they did not know and then could not leave. All John Henry could do was lie on the ground and cry, "They've killed my mother." And soldiers fought and died around him.

Judith Henry had been dead for a while before Jubal Early's brigade arrived on the scene and provoked the subsequent rout of the Federal army. I went to Chinn Ridge, the point from which Early's troops advanced. The road system magnifies the distance between Chinn Ridge and Henry House Hill. But standing on the ridge in December, I could see the Henry House through the bare tree branches and once more appreciated the confined nature of the battlefield.

Actually, it was probably fortunate for the Confederate cause that the simple presence of Early's brigade in position to outflank the Union right had the decisive impact. Those men had had some hard marching that day, and if they had had to go immediately into battle, the results may have been embarrassing. Early ordered a halt at the crest of Chinn Ridge to allow the men to catch their breath. Then he led them forward again across Young's Branch and the Warrenton Turnpike, over Matthews Hill, and to the banks of Bull Run. During this march Early and his men lost sight of their enemies and resorted to following the trail of discarded knapsacks and battlefield debris. When he reached Bull Run, Early was not quite sure what to do; so he called a halt.

Then, while Early pondered what to do, who should ride up but Jefferson Davis, president of the Confederacy. Davis had been chafing in Richmond where he had to be on July 20 to open a session of the Confederate Congress. He traveled to Manassas by train on the day of the battle and had to bargain with the conductor to make him uncouple the cars and take the locomotive alone as close to the battle as Beauregard's headquarters. There Davis secured horses for himself and his staff and rode toward the sound of the firing. As he rode Davis encountered the backwash of battle, men wounded, dazed, and scared, who told the president that the Southern cause was lost. Instead, Davis reached the field in the wake of victory. He was savoring the victory when he encountered Early's unit.

Early had had military training at West Point and experience in the United States Army. But he also was a very direct, unsubtle man. Consequently, when the president rode up while Early was wondering what to do next, he abandoned such niceties as chains-of-command and asked the commander-in-chief for orders. Davis, who took his constitutional title seriously, must have been flattered. He told Early to form a line and wait for someone else's orders. Then Davis rode off to find Beauregard and find out himself what was happening.

Davis and Early were not the only people who were having difficulty sorting out what was happening in the aftermath of triumph. There was confusion on both sides of Bull Run during that late afternoon. And probably nowhere was the confusion greater than about a mile up the Warrenton Turnpike at the bridge over a small tributary of Bull Run called Cub Run. There a bottleneck developed as fleeing Union soldiers vied with frightened civilian spectators in their carriages for passage over the bridge. The confusion became chaos when a battery of Confederate artillery opened on the bridge. The first shot landed squarely in the midst of the squirming mass of people and transformed their panic into hysteria.

The man who fired that first shot was Edmund Ruffin, and he was already well-known for another "first shot." Ruffin was a radical Virginian who had devoted most of his talents and energies since 1845 to the cause of Southern independence. In his mid-sixties, he was a Southern zealot; at Charleston in April, 1861, he had had the honor of jerking the first lanyard on the first direct-fire gun aimed at Fort Sumter. Ruffin had tried to join a South Carolina regiment on the eve of the Manassas campaign, but had found quick-time marches beyond his stamina. Still he was on the field at Manassas. During most of the day he listened to the firing and despaired that his unit was not ordered into action. Finally, Ruffin could stand the suspense no longer and set out alone to find the battle. By chance, he encountered an artillery battery and the chance to ride to the action. And this unit allowed the old man to fire the first shot at the bridge over Cub Run.

I drove up and down US 29/211 several times before I located the Cub Run bridge. It supports four lanes of traffic now and there is no indication that it was briefly so important that July afternoon. Ruffin came to the bridge the next day to survey the damages his shot had caused; he was chagrined to find only three dead bodies nearby. Later, someone told him they had seen seven, and he was happier. Still later, he wrote that there must have been twelve.

It is good that the American people by way of Congress and the National Park Service have hallowed so much of the Bull Run battlefield. But I could not help wishing that the park could annex about an acre around the Cub Run bridge and somehow explain to visitors what happened there. The battlefield now seems to offer a deeper understanding of human valor and folly, tragedy and triumph. At the bridge over Cub Run, visitors might be able to plum the ludicrous depths of human hatred and perhaps such a lesson would be worthwhile.... And it is larger than toy soldiers in a sandbox.

ROANOKE ISLAND AND
MURPHY'S LAW

Some time between 1587 and 1590 the entire English-speaking population of North America vanished. More than one hundred men, seventeen women, and at least one child living in Sir Walter Raleigh's colony
on Roanoke Island in 1587 had disappeared by 1590. Thus began the un-
solved mystery of the "Lost Colony."

Nearly three centuries passed before Roanoke Island again attracted
the world's attention. This time, in February, 1862, the lost colonists at
Roanoke Island were more than 2500 Confederate soldiers, but the facts
of their fate were much less mysterious. The troops were casualties or
prisoners of a massive amphibious assault by their enemies from the
United States. But, there were again unanswered questions about events
on Roanoke Island. A special committee of the Confederate Congress
convened to investigate the "causes and circumstances of the capitulation of Roanoke Island"; in more common language, how and why had
the Southerners so thoroughly bungled?

I wanted to see where this classic debacle occurred—where the Confederacy learned first hand about Murphy's Law. But in order to go
there, I would have to leave a beach. After an idyllic week of undirected
pleasure-seeking, the notion of driving a car anywhere beyond the
Pungo Fish Market seemed absurd. Finally, curiosity triumphed, and
Hunter, who was fifteen, offered to go with me. At fifteen it is possible
to be bored at the beach, and that day the ocean seemed too flat for

worthwhile surfing. So at an early hour of the morning I placed my feet into shoes and set out for Roanoke Island.

As we drove I attempted to explain to Hunter what had happened there in 1862. Although the Confederate congressional committee never discovered it, the "capitulation of Roanoke Island" began in the mind of Union Brigadier General Ambrose E. Burnside. A graduate of West Point and more recently a Rhode Island businessman, Colonel Burnside had led a regiment at Bull Run and earned his star. In the fall of 1861 the full-bearded young general was training raw recruits for Major-General George B. McClellan's new Army of the Potomac. One evening in October Burnside, seeking some more active outlet for his generous energies, pressed upon his commanding general a plan to form a "coast division" with which to invade and occupy land areas and inland waterways along the South Atlantic shoreline. The idea was not exactly novel; within a few weeks the Federals would seize Port Royal, South Carolina, in an operation similar to what Burnside had in mind. Nevertheless McClellan asked Burnside for more details in writing, and perhaps because he had "volunteered," Burnside soon found himself at Annapolis training troops and procuring vessels for his armada.

By December 12 Burnside had 15,000 troops and an adequate but "motley fleet" of sailing vessels, passenger steamers, converted barges, ferry boats, and tugs. The division embarked for four days and sailed on January 9, 1862, for Fort Monroe, Virginia. There the "Burnside Expedition," as it had become known by this time, made rendezvous with its supply ships and put to sea for Cape Hatteras on the night of January 11. When Burnside's 80 vessels reached Hatteras Inlet, 20 naval warships of the North Atlantic Blockading Squadron commanded by Flag-Officer L. M. Goldsborough materialized out of the fog and joined the expedition. Thus by January 13 Burnside's entire amphibious army was hove to at the mouth of Hatteras inlet.

To this point, despite delays and anxious moments, everything had proceeded in rough accord with Burnside's plan. The plan, however, called for eight feet of water in Hatteras Inlet, and nature provided only six. Eventually though nature and naval ingenuity came to Burnside's rescue. At low tide large steamers purposely ran themselves aground on the bar that blocked the inlet. Then sailors rowed out from the ships in small boats carrying anchors. When the ships were firmly anchored on the bar, the swift-running ebb tides washed the sand from under the vessels. As soon as the ships were afloat, crews repeated the process. Finally on January 26 the channel was open, and by February 4 the entire fleet lay at anchor in Pamlico Sound.

While the makeshift fleet waited to pass through the inlet, the troops and crews endured all the discomforts and dangers of midwinter in the North Atlantic. For more than two weeks the ships bobbed about the stormy cape colliding with each other, slipping anchors, and running aground. Three vessels were lost, and two army officers drowned when a surf boat capsized near the bar. After these perils, no doubt members of the expedition had little fear left for the Confederate defenders on Roanoke Island.

Naturally the size and elaborate preparations of the Burnside Expedition could not escape the attention of the Confederacy. Yet even before Burnside began assembling his invasion force and fleet, the Southerners had recognized the military significance of Roanoke Island. The island lies behind North Carolina's outer banks and acts as kind of a geographical plug between Pamlico and Albemarle sounds. Control of Roanoke Island was vital if the Federals were to be kept from moving at will on extensive rivers and inland waterways of North Carolina. In addition the island, because it impeded passage into Albemarle Sound and commanded access to the Dismal Swamp Canal, was the "backdoor to Norfolk." Possession of Roanoke Island was thus crucial to the defense, not only of eastern North Carolina, but Norfolk as well.

Hunter and I became well aware of local coastal geography during our drive that morning. The most direct route to Roanoke Island called for a ferry over Currituck Sound between Knotts Island and Currituck. We were among three vehicles aboard the *Governor J. B. Hunt, Jr.* for

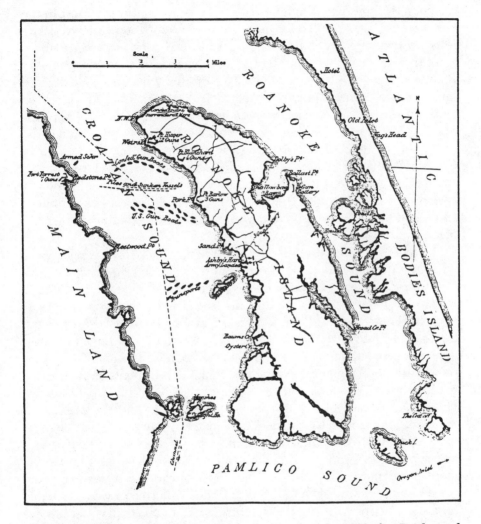

Union operations on Roanoke Island, as mapped in the 1880s for *Battles and Leaders of the Civil War*, a famous series of articles in *The Century Illustrated Monthly Magazine.*

the hour-long passage. From Currituck we drove south, then east to the Outer Banks, then south once more. As we drove we encountered delays for road construction, then delays in traffic. It took us three hours to drive those eighty miles, and by the time we crossed the causeway onto Roanoke Island we had some small feeling for what Burnside's troops must have felt after finally reaching their destination.

About the time Burnside's armada left Annapolis there were approximately 1500 North Carolina state troops on Roanoke Island under the command of Colonel H. M. Shaw. To support the land troops Navy Captain William F. Lynch commanded a fleet of two sidewheel steamers, six tiny gunboats, and a floating artillery battery. Neither Shaw nor Lynch were satisfied with these resources; neither believed the Confederacy could hold Roanoke Island against a determined effort to take the place.

Confederate occupation of the island began back in August of 1861, when the Union seized Fort Hatteras and Fort Clark covering the passage from ocean to sound at Hatteras Inlet. Confederate Major-General Benjamin Huger at that time included the island in his Department of Norfolk. Huger, an "old army" South Carolinian, then began playing the "game" of departmental command. He tried to have the boundaries of his department gerrymandered to place Roanoke Island outside of his responsibility. The concept of geographical departments seemed quite sound to the Confederacy in 1861; to resist invasion the War Office divided the "front" into geographical departments and assigned commanders and troops to each. When invasion came, the Southerners depended upon departmental commanders to borrow or lend troops and supplies to support an endangered sector. Otherwise the departments were more or less autonomous. Trouble was, the departments too often became "empires" and the War Office too often proved incapable of moving troops with speed and efficiency from one department to another. The system was too inflexible, and Roanoke Island was a classic example of its inadequacy.

Roanoke Island and Murphy's Law

By November Huger, who admittedly had his hands full in Norfolk, managed to contract the limits of his department so as to exclude Roanoke Island. But in early January, while Burnside was loading his troop transports, the War Office redrew the boundaries of the Department of Norfolk, and again Huger assumed responsibility for Roanoke Island. Judah P. Benjamin, then taking his turn as Secretary of War, not only gave Huger Roanoke; he also gave him Brigadier General Henry A. Wise and the Wise "Legion."

Wise was an excellent Democratic politician; he had been Governor of Virginia and through his son O. Jennings Wise controlled the Richmond *Enquirer,* the Southern "Democratic Bible." Wise was also an ardent Confederate; he had led the "Southern rights" movement in Virginia and formed his brigade-sized "legion" for the cause. But Wise was no general, however much he tried to be. After he had campaigned with little success in Western Virginia during the Summer of 1861, he became ill. When Wise recovered and demanded command of the legion, Benjamin tried to find a backwater of the war in which to place him. Roanoke Island seemed perfect at the time; so in the latter part of December Wise received his orders, and Huger received Wise, his legion, and the island.

Unfortunately the legion was still in transit to Richmond and would continue to be so for some time. Thus Wise, when he assumed his new command on January 7, added only himself and his staff to the island's defenders. Even a soldier as inexperienced as Wise realized that the Confederate forces on Roanoke were in no condition to defend themselves.

The succession of commands and commanders on the island had made attempts to fortify the place, but the net result of this activity was ludicrous. The enemy, be he Burnside or anyone else, was certain to assault Roanoke Island from the south across Pamlico Sound. Yet the Confederates had constructed forts on the extreme northern end of the island. The water passage around Roanoke was narrowest off the southern tip; but the Confederates were trying to block Croatan Sound (between the island and the mainland) at a point where the sound was more than three miles wide.

Some engineers in Norfolk had determined that the current at the southern end of the island was too swift to plant obstructions there. The engineers, of course, never visited Roanoke Island. To his credit Colonel Shaw recognized the dilemma. However, Shaw had been unable to get sufficient rations for his North Carolinians, much less train them or collect the necessary arms and ammunition to improve the situation. Captain Lynch of the navy was an energetic man. However Lynch was severely hampered by the want of ships, weapons, ammunition, and experience. To understate, Wise was displeased with the condition of his command.

Hunter and I drove through Manteo, the principal town on the island, and went first to Fort Raleigh from which the first colonists had disappeared and where the National Park Service maintains a historic site. Quite understandably, the emphasis at Fort Raleigh was upon the lost colony; however a ranger told us that one of her colleagues knew what there was to know about the Civil War on Roanoke Island. That ranger told us that no Civil War remains remained; just about everything was under water. He directed us to where the Confederate forts had been and said that at low tide some of the obstructions in Croatan Sound were visible. We followed his directions and found some low mounds on a small point; but the tide was high. Thus far Hunter and I were doing about as well as Henry A. Wise.

Wise the politician determined he could best improve the situation on Roanoke by doing what he did well. He left the island and hurried to Norfolk, then Richmond, to politick for troops, supplies, and equipment. Before he departed, though, Wise the general gave instructions to Shaw which in essence directed him to persist in the earlier follies of Roanoke's defense—improve the fortifications at Pork and Weirs points on the northern end of the island and continue sinking that row of piles across three miles of Croatan Sound.

At Norfolk and Richmond, Wise found he could accomplish little. Both Huger and Benjamin were concerned with his plight and promised all the support they were able to give. But there just was not enough support to go around. The unpleasant fact was that the Confederacy was desperately undermanned and outgunned; perhaps more so at this time than ever again until 1865. Materiel purchased in Europe had not yet arrived; Southern ordnance works had not yet begun to produce in quantity; the one-year enlistments of a majority of the Southern army were about over; and reverses in the West had drained the War Department of vital arms and men. Wise did expedite, to some degree, the arrival of his legion on Roanoke and secure sympathy and promises from his higher headquarters. He was, however, less than optimistic when he returned to his command on January 30.

Meanwhile on January 20 Lynch discovered the lead elements of Burnside's force making their way into Pamlico Sound. Realizing that his force was too weak and small to give battle, Lynch returned to Roanoke Island and reported to Secretary of the Navy Stephen R. Mallory. Lynch stated that Roanoke was doomed and the army was at fault; Mallory had better be ready to dodge blame for the impending disaster.

A few days later Wise returned to the island, but not for long. He established his headquarters at Nags Head on the outer banks. Then on February 1 Wise took to his bed with a severe attack of pleurisy. Between spasms of coughing blood, Wise issued orders to Shaw and to the men of his legion which had managed to reach Roanoke Island. With these troops was the general's son Captain O. Jennings Wise. Despite these eleventh-hour exertions, the island's defenses were in no condition to receive the Burnside expedition when it steamed up Pamlico Sound on February 7.

Burnside had fairly accurate maps and charts of the area, and he also had good advice about landing sites from a black refugee from Roanoke. The Confederates had even left channel buoys in tact. Admiral Goldsborough's warships made first contact with the Rebels at about 11:30 on the morning of the seventh. Shore batteries at Pork and Weirs points opened on the Union flotilla to little effect. Likewise Lynch's gunboats came under Federal fire before their own guns could reach the enemy.

Union vessels managed to sink one Southern gunboat and disable another before Lynch, his ammunition exhausted, broke off the engagement. Because the Confederates had left an opening in the row of pilings across Croatan Sound, the obstruction was all but useless. Under cover of darkness on the evening of the seventh, Lynch took his impotent fleet to Elizabeth City in search of ammunition.

Meanwhile at about 3:30 in the afternoon Federal troops began debarking on the sandy beach of Ashby's Harbor near the center of the island. They met no resistance from the Southerners who were fighting fires ignited by the naval shelling and preparing to make a stand near the center of the island. By midnight 10,000 troops were ashore at Ashby's Harbor. The Federals spent a restless, chilly night, and after a month aboard ships no doubt most of the men had to regain their "land legs."

Colonel Shaw's Confederates were also uncomfortable on the night of the seventh. Many of the island's defenders spent the night in the marshes bordering a low hill where they would make their stand. Shaw brought up three artillery pieces and placed them in a hastily constructed redoubt. Near dawn on February 8, Shaw realized that he had no one in his command who knew how to fire the pieces. The frantic colonel requested help from Wise, and a captain sent over from Nags Head was still giving lessons when the Union advance began.

About seven o'clock the battle began. Burnside had divided his force into three brigades; one of these confronted the redoubt while the other two picked their way through the marshes on either side. By 12:20 the battle was over. At the redoubt the Southerners had exhausted their ammunition, and the Federals had crushed the Rebel right flank. Most of the vanquished surrendered in place; there was nowhere to retreat. Roughly 2500 Confederates were prisoners; O. Jennings Wise son of the general was among 24 dead. Union casualties numbered 264.

After Roanoke Island Burnside exploited his victory and pressed on to capture New Bern. Wise was left to grieve for his son and to try to explain the debacle. In the end he combined the two tasks and sought revenge from Huger and Benjamin for the predicament in which they had left him.

The original lost colonists on Roanoke Island left only the word CROATAN carved on a tree for investigators to ponder. Wise who had little else to do with his time furnished the Congressional investigating committee 143 pages of venom on his loss of Roanoke Island. The committee concurred with Wise's indictment and saddled Huger and Benjamin with full responsibility for the disaster. Amid the myriad mistakes made by nearly everyone involved on the Southern side, such a verdict was indeed unjust. The committee merely compounded the comedy of errors. Everything and everyone involved had contributed to the disaster. The departmental command system, "political" generals, interservice rivalry, paucity of war materiel, lack of a navy, military bureaucracy, and human stupidity all played a role. The Congressional committee then transformed a military debacle into a political crisis. And in the end the Confederates were left with no more than what Sir Walter Raleigh had retained on Roanoke Island.

On the way out of town, we stopped at the site of the battle on February 8, 1862, now a very congested intersection. En route back to the beach we decided against the Currituck Ferry and wore out three road maps trying to return to the beach without going by way of downtown Norfolk.

We had not had a bad time; Hunter was good company. By late afternoon we were cooling off in the Atlantic Ocean at Sandbridge Beach. Still, I could not help but be apologetic for dragging Hunter over lots of miles to see very little. But Hunter refused my apology. And with the refreshing wisdom of a fifteen-year-old he said, "What did you expect? When you go looking for the remains of a battle like Roanoke Island, the most appropriate thing you can find is nothing."

ART, LIFE, AND SHILOH

"Shiloh" the short story by Bobbie Ann Mason is about Norma Jean and Leroy Moffit who are thirty-four years old and Mabel Beasly who is Norma Jean's mother. They live pretty meaningless, vapid lives in a town in western Kentucky during this present time. Mabel admits that she is, "just waiting for time to pass," and Leroy is too, although he senses rather than says it. Norma Jean is trying. She tries self-help fads, and she tries adult-education courses at the local community college—"It's something to do."

These people are troubled and frustrated for a number of reasons. One of the reasons they are troubled and frustrated is history, or the lack of it rather, the rootless, aimless detachment from time and place that afflicts many middle American moderns. Norma Jean, Leroy, and Mabel are cultural amnesiacs, victims of "Shopping Mall Chic" of which a needlepoint *Star Trek* pillow cover is an artifact.

Long ago on her honeymoon Mabel visited Shiloh battlefield, and she urges Leroy to take Norma Jean there in an effort to preserve their marriage. "Take her on down to Shiloh. Y'all need to get out together, stir a little." Later, "I always thought Shiloh was the prettiest place," she says, "so full of history." And finally Norma Jean agrees to go.

Leroy expected the place to look like a golf course. For Leroy, war is "a board game with plastic soldiers"; the cemetery looks to him like a subdivision site. He can only compare the Confederate surprise attack to a drug bust that took place in a bowling alley back home. When he tries to reflect upon his own personal past, he finds that, "he is leaving out the insides of history." "History was always just names and dates to him."

Art, Life, and Shiloh

Similarly "the real inner workings of a marriage, like most of history, have escaped him."

Norma Jean seems numb during most of their visit. Finally after a picnic lunch near the battlefield cemetery, she announces that she wants to leave Leroy. She knows what happened at Shiloh in April of 1862 no better than Leroy. But Shiloh stands for history (among other things); it is a special place. And it is there that Norma Jean chooses to try to come to terms with her past in the present.

Bobbie Ann Mason who wrote *Shiloh and Other Stories* (as well as *In Country*) had more than history in mind when she wrote this incredibly compelling story. For me, though, "Shiloh" is a parable about history and places where history happened. From one perspective, at least, it is a story about the "insides of history" and a place "so full of history."

Here are the "names and dates" of Shiloh. On April 6, 1862, a Confederate army of 40,000 men commanded by Albert Sidney Johnston attacked an almost equal number of Federals commanded by Ulysses S. Grant near Shiloh Church. The attack caught the Federals by surprise and almost drove them into the Tennessee River. But the Union troops rallied, the Southern assault stalled, Johnston suffered a mortal wound, and his successor in command P. G. T. Beauregard called a halt late in the day. During the night Grant regrouped and found reinforcements. On April 7 the Northern army counterattacked and recovered the ground lost the previous day, and Beauregard led his Confederates from the field toward Corinth, Mississippi.

Those are the essential facts of the battle. But the essence of the events, "the insides of history," was (among other things) the human drama that took place at Shiloh. Here are samples of human drama for which Shiloh was the stage.

Johnston planned to march his army from Corinth to Shiloh on April 3 and attack Grant's army on April 4 in the morning. But the march took three days instead of one, and the Southern soldiers seemed determined to announce their intentions to their enemies. They fired their rifles to make sure they worked. They shouted to one another, blew bugles, beat drums, and built large fires despite orders to the contrary. The staff officer who composed the orders for the campaign used as his guide the orders of Napoleon—at Waterloo. A prudent general would have aborted the entire plan and returned to Corinth. But Johnston continued his march and dared to make his attack. "Tonight," he said as his men were forming for the assault, "we will water our horses in the Tennessee River!"

The greatest surprise about the Southern attack was that it was in fact a surprise. A series of circumstances allowed the Confederates to advance undetected until they launched their assault. Then one nervous Union colonel decided what he should do only when one of his soldiers burst into camp with a bloody arm screaming, "Get in line! The Rebels are coming!" William Tecumseh Sherman commanded the Northern division the Southern army struck first. His first response to a report from one of his subordinates was to say, "You must be badly scared over there," which sounds like nondirective psychotheraphy (Carl Rogers); but Sherman probably intended sarcasm. A short time later Sherman saw the advancing columns and exclaimed, "My God, we are attacked!"

For a time Johnston's men enjoyed a relatively easy advance through the Federal camps. But when the Federals recovered from the initial shock and surprise, fighting became fierce and terrible. One Northern soldier remembered that in the midst of the noise and chaos of exploding shells and screaming men, a rabbit ran out of some bushes and huddled next to him as he lay on the firing line. Another soldier sought refuge behind a large tree; then another came to stand behind him; a third man joined them; then a fourth, a fifth, and soon a long file of soldiers had formed behind the tree, while an officer, for no logical reason, paced up and down the file as though he were on a parade ground.

Part of the battlefield was a peach orchard. Indeed the peach trees were in bloom on April 6, and petals shaken by the concussion of battle floated down upon blood and bodies, as if nature were making some sort of statement about the violence and killing in this place.

To the peach orchard in the afternoon came General Sidney Johnston to rally a regiment of his troops to charge the Northern line once more. He rode his horse up and down the line of men, reached over and touched their bayonets, and shouted, "These will do the work...." Then he turned his mount toward the Federal line, called out, "I will lead you!" and started forward with the troops.

Inspired by the commanding general, the regiment broke the Union line and drove the Northern troops back upon a portion of their line that had become a stronghold—the Hornets' Nest, so called because of the fury and numbers of bullets flying there. When Johnston returned from the charge his uniform had been torn in several places by enemy fire. "They didn't trip me up that time!" he said with emotion. Then he began sending members of his staff with messages to his subordinates in various parts of the field. He sent them all away on one errand or another until he was alone.

Isham G. Harris, the Governor of Tennessee, was serving as a volunteer aide to Johnston that day. When Harris returned from delivering a message for Johnston, he discovered the general about to fall off his horse. Johnston was pale, weak, and dazed. Harris held him on his horse and ushered the general to a place of greater safely in a nearby ravine. He then helped Johnston down and began trying to find a wound. Eventually Harris located a hole in Johnston's leg just above his knee; a bullet had cut the artery, and Johnston was bleeding to death. The Governor did not know about pressure points to stop arterial bleeding. And neither did Johnston's chief of staff who arrived on the scene soon after Harris found the wound. Perhaps it was already too late. But because Harris lacked the First Aid skills now possessed by an average Boy Scout, the Governor could only bend over the general and repeat, "Johnston, do you know me? Johnston, do you know me?" while Johnston died.

Throughout the day Northern troops were moving. They recoiled and ran from the Southern assault; they marched to the aid of their comrades in threatened portions of the battle line; and they crowded ashore from steamboats on the Tennessee River. During the morning a battered regiment stumbling to the rear passed fresh troops marching to the battlefront. "Fill your canteens boys!" called the colonel of the broken unit, "Some of you will be in hell before night and you'll need the water!"

When reinforcements began arriving from across the Tennessee late in the day, they found the landing crowded with stragglers and walking wounded, men who had quit the battle. William "Bull" Nelson who was over six feet tall and weighed 300 pounds commanded the division about to come ashore. He mounted his horse while still aboard the steamboat, drew his sword, and jammed his spurs into his mount. The horse (which must have been quite an animal) jumped over the gunwale and carried Nelson into the mass of milling men on shore. "Damn your souls!" Nelson bellowed, "If you won't fight, get out of the way, and let men come here who will!"

Among the stragglers was an army chaplain who was doing his best to inspire the men to return to the fight. His best, though, sounded pretty weak, "Rally, men, rally and we may yet be saved! O rally, for god and your country's sake, rally...." One of "Bull" Nelson's subordinate officers, taking a cue from his chieftain, hollered at the chaplain, "Shut up, you Goddamned old fool, or I'll break your head! Get out of the way!"

P. G. T. Beauregard who succeeded Johnston in command of the Confederates did not know that Federal reinforcements had arrived when he ordered his army to suspend the attack for that day. He sent a telegram to Richmond, "After a severe, battle of ten hours, thanks be to the Almighty, we have gained a complete victory...."

Beauregard did not know Ulysses S. Grant either. When asked during the night if he wanted plans made for a retreat, Grant responded, "No, I purpose to attack at daylight and whip them!" Sherman found Grant standing under a tree in the rain holding a lantern. "Well, Grant, we've had the devil's own day, haven't we?" Grant answered, "Yes, lick 'em tomorrow, though."

Grant and his army did "lick'em" the next day. Indeed, after hard fighting on April 7, one of Beauregard's subordinates said to him, "General, do you not think our troops are very much in the condition of a lump of sugar, thoroughly soaked with water, but yet preserving its original shape, though ready to dissolve? Would it not be judicious to get away with what we have?" Beauregard must have accepted the sugar lump metaphor, because he did break off the combat and retreat to keep from getting licked anymore.

As the Confederates withdrew, some of them had to fight a rearguard action to protect their comrades. One of the units called upon to slow the Federal pursuit was a regiment of Tennessee cavalry (350 men) commanded by Nathan Bedford Forrest. As Sherman's division of Federals picked its way forward near a place called Fallen Timbers, Forrest formed up his horsemen on a ridge which lay across the path of the advance. The Southerners were outnumbered five or six to one. Forrest charged.

A Union regiment spread out as skirmishers led Sherman's division forward. Conventional wisdom and common sense dictated that Forrest and his cavalry drive the scattered skirmishers back upon the main body of Federal troops and then make a hasty exit. This would compel Sherman to halt his march and deploy his troops for battle, and these activities would cost him time, and that was Forrest's mission. The Southern horsemen carried out their risky task; they drove the Federal skirmishers to flight and scattered a regiment of Federal horsemen as well.

But Forrest lost control—of himself. He continued to scream, "Charge!" and kept galloping straight at the oncoming masses of Northern infantry. Forrest's men had better sense; they turned back and withdrew to their ridge. So Forrest charged alone. He rode headlong into the ranks of an infantry brigade.

He was slashing with his saber, while his enemies surrounded him. He absorbed a pistol bullet in the hip fired at point-blank range. Men tried to grab hold of him and pull him to the ground. Miraculously Forrest remained on his horse and alive. When the momentum of his charge slowed, he wheeled his mount and charged back through the Union ranks toward his men. As he plunged again through the blue gauntlet, he grabbed a federal soldier by the collar and hauled the man aboard his horse as a shield. When he broke free of the Federals, Forrest dumped his shield on the ground and rejoined his command.

Forrest's frenzy that afternoon built his legend. And after Forrest's charge Sherman simply stopped his pursuit and returned to Shiloh.

Shiloh was the bloodiest battle to that time ever in the Western Hemisphere—about 20,000 men dead or wounded—about 3,400 men killed in battle and 2,000 more mortally wounded. One of the young men who died from his wounds was a Confederate named Will Pope. As he died, Pope asked his friend Johnny Green, "Johnny, if a boy dies for his country the glory is his forever isn't it?" Surely there is some cruel irony in the coincidence that on the same day (April 7), in 1775, Dr. Samuel Johnson proclaimed, "Patriotism is the last refuge of a scoundrel."

Albert Sidney Johnston, Napoleon, William Tecumseh Sherman, a scared rabbit, a large tree, peach blossoms, Isham Harris, full canteens, William "Bull" Nelson, an insipid chaplain, P. G. T. Beauregard, Ulysses S. Grant, a sugar lump, Nathan Bedford Forrest, and Will Pope— these were some of the actors and props in the human drama of a great battle. If nothing else, Shiloh is a series of stories about people and human response in crisis.

But what about the place? I knew about the events and incidents of Shiloh, the "insides" of the event, from the insides of books (especially James Lee McDonough's *Shiloh-in Hell Before Night*). I wanted to go to the ground and see if there were transcendence between history and the place. Was Shiloh, in fact, "so full of history"? Was the place important enough to be the thing that drove Bobbie Ann Mason's story?

I set out on a sparkling September morning and about an hour into the drive reached I 285, the perimeter highway around Atlanta. I had successfully avoided the morning traffic rush hour; but on I 285 there is always congested motion. This was present tense life in several fast lanes.

On both sides of this multilane highway, Atlanta boomed and

bloomed at the same time. Steel, concrete, and glass shapes rose from the trees like monstrous solid geometry problems. And huge cranes planted at intervals were busy filling the suburban skyline with more branch office art. Modern angles were now competing with postmodern curves in the newest of Souths.

In my mind I imagined the opening sequences of a movie—perhaps a variation on *The Big Chill*. I was one of the principal characters in the film, and here I was zipping among BMWs, Jaguars, and Volvos. The rock montage on the radio established the beat as big and up. The camera captured the motion of the Interstate and the glitter of shaped glass that flanked the road. And as the credits flashed like oversized turn-signals on each side of the big screen, the audience would know that something chic and exciting was about to happen.

Then I realized that I had been imagining life that imitated art, and not very fine art at that. Art is supposed to reflect life—not life, art. I was acting as mindlessly as Bobbie Ann Mason's Leroy Moffit when he imagined war as "a board game with plastic soldiers."

The rest of the trip was less introspective—Cartersville, Dalton, Chattanooga, Sewanee, Winchester (Skip's Grill bacon cheeseburger) Pulaski, Savannah (Tennessee), and finally Shiloh in the late afternoon. I looked around briefly, decided to spend the night in Corinth, Mississippi, and approach Shiloh from the same direction Johnston's Confederate army had come in April, 1862.

Next morning I drove the distance it had taken the Confederates three days to march in twenty-eight minutes. And I encountered a large truck loaded with larger logs and a couple of Sunday drivers on Wednesday en route. The countryside was rural—modest houses, three fallout shelters, and countless satellite dishes. The battlefield park offers little contrast from its surroundings, and the National Park Service owns just about all of the land on which the battle took place. The fields, woods, and roads are nearly the same as they were when the battle occurred.

One of the best ways I have found to be a tourist is to go running in the area that interests me. I have, for instance, run the Battery in

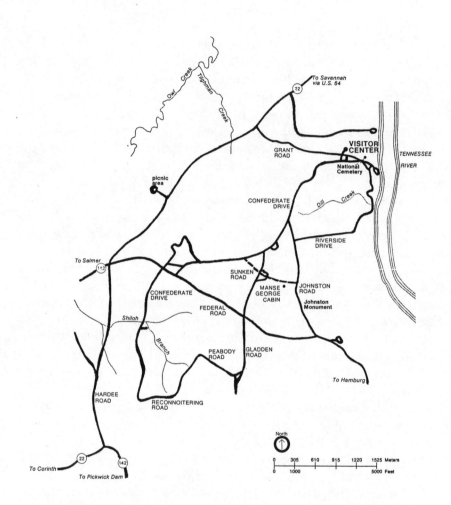

Shiloh National Military Park.

Art, Life, and Shiloh

Charleston, Monument Avenue in Richmond, and some sections of the streetcar line in New Orleans. So I decided to run Shiloh—or at least six miles of the ten-mile driving circuit of the battlefield.

For the most part the terrain is fairly flat, and what slopes there are are gentle. I renewed my appreciation of how confusing the road network and the interspersed fields and woods could be. Major General Lew Wallace, who later wrote *Ben Hur*, commanded a Union division at Shiloh; but Wallace and his 7,000 troops never found the action on the first day of the battle, and no one has ever with certainty determined why. Wallace himself during the last years of his life returned to the battlefield frequently and walked over the ground as though he were trying to resolve the riddle. On April 6, 1862, Wallace may have been the victim of garbled orders. But he also contended with a confusing landscape and road system. Even with the benefit of paved roads, signs, and labels, I could understand Wallace's quandary.

After the run, I cooled down for awhile and then returned to several sites on the battlefield to examine them more carefully. I went to the place near the peach orchard where Governor Harris discovered Johnston reeling on his horse. Years later Harris returned to Shiloh and identified the oak tree under which he had found the general. Now the tree is a dead stump supported by metal brackets. Harris also established the spot in the nearby ravine to which he had taken Johnston and where Johnston soon after died. The ravine was cool and quiet when I went there. But I could imagine the consternation in that place at 2:30 in the afternoon on the first day of the battle.

I had read about Bloody Pond and had seen pictures of it. Yet Bloody Pond never made much impression on me until I went there. It was simply a shallow pool in some quiet woods. During the battle the pond offered relief to wounded soldiers from both armies by turns. Men came to the pond to drink and to cleanse their wounds. As the fighting became more intense, men and horses died there, and the accumulated outpouring of blood turned the water red. The light and growth in the water made Bloody Pond appear burnt orange to me. But I could easily imag-

Bloody Pond today.

ine burnt orange as red and wounded men coming to the water for relief. Add to this the religious symbolism of water and some New
Testament pool imagery (Bethzatha/Bethesda), and Bloody Pond became indeed a meaningful part of the battle drama.

I stood on both sides of the open ground in front of the sunken road
and rail fence that defined the Hornets' Nest. First I was a Federal soldier, watching the tree line for the next wave of frenzied, screaming
Rebels to emerge. Then I was a Confederate staring at the field I would

The Hornet's Nest today.

have to cross while concealed men tried to shoot me down. The sunken road is still sunken, though not as much so, I suspect, as on the day of the battle. The worn down ground formed a natural trench line and, with the fence, protected Federal defenders—until the Southerners opened upon them with 62 pieces of field artillery. But the men who huddled together (with rabbits) in this patch of woods stopped the Southern advance long enough for Grant to form another defense line behind them. And because the Confederates continued to spend time and blood hurling themselves at the Hornet's Nest, Grant was able to save his army. Finally 2100 Federal survivors surrendered themselves and this stronghold. But by the time they did, the Southern assault had stalled for good.

When I went down to Pittsburg Landing, I found grass and concrete holding the slope down to the Tennessee River. Some men in motorboats were fishing for catfish in the river, and three generations of a Tennessee family were wandering about the site. I tried to picture several thousand dispirited soldiers milling about this place and "Bull" Nelson bellowing at the men as he rode his horse into the throng. This was definitely a bottleneck; so many men in this small space threatened to prevent the arriving reinforcements from even coming ashore, much less marching up the hill and into Grant's line of battle. The Union army needed Nelson or someone like him to open the way for the fresh troops. The crisis of the late afternoon of April 6, 1862, remained confined in my imagining, though; the closest thing to a crisis I actually saw at Pittsburg Landing occurred when a small boy forgot where he had left his sneakers.

Because the Federal army remained on the field when the battle ended, Grant's troops had to dispose of the dead bodies that lay there after two days of fighting. Burial details dug large trenches and, in many cases, piled the remains of friends and foes together. Later the bodies of Federal troops were removed to the battlefield cemetery; the Confederates remained in the trenches. I saw a couple of the burial trenches—one contained more than 700 bodies. Looking at the elongated mound surrounded by concrete and cannon balls, I could only think of films of mass graves at Auschwitz and other Nazi death camps—corpses tossed on top of corpses while bulldozers waited to cover the monstrous crime. Perhaps it was appropriate to associate even this battle, so primitive by modern standards, with "crimes against humanity." Studying war was fast making me a pacifist.

Tom Connelly had said that Shiloh was an "eerie" place. He once wrote about summer evenings when he and his brothers wandered about the battlefield, "half fearful of the ghosts of the 23,000 casualties who everyone said roamed the field by night." I did not hang around after dark, and it did seem strange to see so many monuments and markers in the midst of otherwise ordinary forests and fields. Yet I did not consider Shiloh eerie.

Shiloh, however, was a special place, because of what had happened there. I reconfirmed that I was not an aficionado of battlefields; I suspected as much after visiting Manassas/Bull Run. But like Manassas/Bull Run, Shiloh was well worth the trip.

Being on the scene and knowing what had happened there made a difference. That difference was probably not as pronounced as the difference between looking at pictures of Michelangelo's *David* and seeing *David* in Florence or between reading Shakespeare and attending a performance of *Othello*. I found the difference between reading a good narrative of the battle and going to the battlefield similar to the difference between watching a baseball game on television and going to the ballpark or between listening to a record or tape and attending a live concert.

I realized that whenever I had read about Shiloh or any other historical event I had formed mental images of the action in my mind's eye. Perhaps the nearest analogy would be a series of color slides advancing in my head—a collection of imaginary pictures that flashed before my consciousness while I read, for example, about the fury in the Hornets' Nest or Albert Sidney Johnston's final minutes of life. The opportunity to walk within the Hornets' Nest, to stand in that ravine where Johnston died, made those mental images more accurate and signficantly more vivid.

Thoughts about images and imaginary pictures recalled the dialogue I had had with myself on the Atlanta perimeter highway about life, art, and history. And the long drive toward home afforded plenty of time to renew the conversation and extend my thinking.

"History," I said to myself, "is life—experience."

"But," I responded to myself, "history is also art. It is stories, books, articles, films, television programs, and more about the experience of life."

"So," I concluded with myself, "history is a creative, interpretive response to experience. It is, or ought to be, art which springs from life and at the same time attempts to expand and deepen an understanding of life."

And so I returned to Bobbie Ann Mason and "Shiloh." The story is art about life and history. The characters in the story go to Shiloh, and the place "so full of history" compels them to confront life. Under very different circumstances, the same thing had happened to me.

OZYMANDIAS AND FORT PULASKI

Fort Pulaski is an unnatural place. It is located on Cockspur Island at the mouth of the Savannah River and once controlled access to the port of Savannah and interior waterways. Cockspur Island is man-made, the product of dredging channels in the Savannah River. A young engineer officer fresh from West Point named Robert E. Lee began his career here in 1829 working on a drainage system to stabilize the island. Construction of the fort consumed eighteen years, 1 million nineteenth-century dollars, and 25 million bricks. And to get to this man-made fort on the artificial island, I drove across a man-made causeway and down a highway imposed by people and machines upon a salt marsh.

I first went to Fort Pulaski simply to see the place. But while there I relearned one of the most compelling "lessons" that history has to teach—about the persistence of change in human affairs.

Certainly the French saying that "the more things change, the more they remain the same," is valid, and surely history reveals continuity across the centuries. But paradoxically change and continuity seem both to be historical constants.

When completed in 1847, Fort Pulaski was supposed to be "as strong as the Rocky Mountains." During the Civil War the fort proved to be about as stable as one Cascade Range mountain—Mount St. Helens. Pulaski illustrates the folly of stability and security, and the struggle for possession of the fort is a fascinating story.

Even before Georgia seceded from the Union, state troops took possession of the fort, and soon thereafter the Confederate army garrisoned the bastion. Then in November of 1861 the Federals captured Hilton

Head just to the north, and the Confederates began preparing in earnest to defend Pulaski. Robert E. Lee returned to Savannah and for a while directed preparations for defense of the city. About Fort Pulaski Lee had few immediate worries. He warned that the garrison might be surrounded and besieged; but Lee seemed to agree with Chief Engineer of the United States Army Joseph G. Totten who proclaimed that Pulaski "could not be reduced in a month's firing with any number of guns of manageable calibers."

Understandably Colonel Charles Olmstead who commanded the fort confined his preparations to stocking up supplies and moving some of his guns to answer an attack from the land as well as from the sea. Meanwhile Union General Quincy Gilmore was busy trying to do what men more knowledgeable and experienced than he had pronounced impossible. Gilmore directed the landing of 33 big guns on Tybee Island and the transport of these cumbersome weapons across 2½ miles of sand and marsh to a sand ridge within one to two miles of Fort Pulaski.

The guns, some of which weighed 17,000 pounds—about the same as 62 midsize refrigerators or more than 4 Lincoln Continental automobiles—came ashore on small boats at high tide. The men then waited until low tide and the firmest beach possible to drag the pieces above the high-water line. Next they winched the guns onto very large wooden platforms and then raised and lashed each end of the platforms to the undersides of carts. In effect the Federals constructed a temporary wagon under each gun for the journey overland and into Gilmore's firing line.

But, although the soldiers also built makeshift causeways over the marsh, the wagons quite often sank into the mud up to the hubs of the wheels. When this happened the men had to unload the guns and wrestle them forward on planks until they reached firmer ground. No less than 250 men strained at the ropes of the heavier pieces. They strained in the dark and in silence, too, forbidden to curse above a whisper, to conceal Gilmore's intentions from the Confederates in Fort Pulaski.

While some of the Federals were hauling the guns, others prepared

An aerial view of Fort Pulaski in the 1950s. Courtesy of the National Park Service.

positions for the pieces on the low ridge of sand overlooking the water and the fort. They took considerable care to alter the outline of the topography as little as possible and gradually added brush and bushes to the sand ridge until they had formed a screen between themselves and the fort. Very early in the Federal occupation of Tybee Island, the Confederates had demonstrated the need for such stealth. Two soldiers had stood on the point of sand nearest the fort and shouted challenges at the Southerners. The Confederates answered with an artillery round which cut one of the Federals in half.

Yet even though the Confederates knew or suspected what Gilmore's men were doing, there seemed no reason for concern. Conventional wisdom dictated that the fort was safe. Indeed one of the Federal officers said that he hoped the details of this operation would never be known abroad. European military experts would have a loud laugh, he believed, if they ever learned of this folly. Gilmore had ignored just about every rule of military engineering.

Finally on April 10, 1862, more than four months after Gilmore had made his first reconnaissance on Tybee, the Union guns and gunners were ready. On that day the Federals sent a formal demand to Olmstead that he surrender Fort Pulaski. Olmstead responded simply that he was there "to defend the fort, not to surrender it." Consequently at 8:15 A.M. the bombardment commenced and continued throughout the day.

Ironically the Federals' great 13-inch mortars and monstrous Columbiads, guns which had been most difficult to move across the sand and marsh mud, were essentially ineffective. Yet by one o'clock on April 9, it was apparent that Fort Pulaski was doomed.

Gilmore had installed rifled artillery that fired exploding shells (instead of solid shot) on his firing line. The Parrot and James rifles had spiraled bores (grooves inside the barrels) that caused the shells to spin as they fired improving range and accuracy. The effect was similar to throwing a football, instead of a basketball, at a distant target. As the conical shells of the rifled artillery penetrated the fort and exploded, they gradually blasted holes in the thick brick walls.

During the night of the tenth the firing slowed apace, but resumed the next morning. Naturally the Confederates fired back, but Olmstead's gunners were unable to disable their tormentors. By noon on April 11, the Federals had opened two gaping holes in the side of the fort and soon after sent three shots into the Confederate powder magazine. Olmstead realized his situation was hopeless and with good reason feared that he and his men might very well be blown up by their own gunpowder.

Ozymandias and Fort Pulaski

Accordingly at 2:00 P.M. on April 11, he ran up a white flag and prepared to surrender Fort Pulaski.

In 30 hours rifled artillery had rendered obsolete the 25 million bricks and 18 years of work at Fort Pulaski. Olmstead and his 384 defenders at the fort learned a hard lesson about the persistence of change and the folly of security.

All I could think of was Shelley's "Ozymandias," the sonnet about the pedestal in the desert which reads:

"My name is Ozymandias, King of Kings:
Look on my works, ye Mighty and despair!"

But the poem continues:

Nothing beside remains. Round the decay
Of that colossal wreck, boundless and bare
The lone and level sands stretch far away.

The only constant is flux. But those who taught this lesson did not seem to learn it. Within six weeks after they occupied Fort Pulaski, the Yankees had repaired the breech in the wall—to make the fort safe again.

RIDING WITH A CALCULATING CAVALIER

Once upon a time I set out to write a biography of J.E.B. Stuart. Biography is one way to attain a broader and deeper understanding of the human condition. Because such things as "human condition" and "understanding" were at stake, I took my task as a biographer quite seriously—as it happened, a bit too seriously. I was determined to "get inside of" Stuart, and used that *cliché* as though I had first thought of it.

After I had completed a few draft chapters about Stuart's early life, one of my sons (whose name resembles mine) asked to read what I had written. I asked him to tell me if I had "gotten inside of" Stuart, because I was concerned that I had not. He had several comments when I finished reading the chapters. But the most helpful concerned my concern for Stuart's interior. "No," he said, "you have not 'gotten inside of' Stuart." Then he added, "you can't get inside of another person. The best you can do is get *beside* a person, and you have done that with Stuart so far." He was right. And when I abandoned my pretentiousness about what a biographer can and cannot do, I enjoyed Stuart a lot more.

In the course of my effort to "get beside" Jeb Stuart, I undertook to retrace the route of his famous "ride around McClellan" of June, 1862. I drove the hundred miles that Stuart rode around the Union army threatening Richmond. This was Stuart's first great cavalry raid. The expedition brought him instant fame then, and later historian Douglas S. Freeman aptly entitled a chapter about the event "J.E.B. Stuart Earns His Plume."

Riding with a Calculating Cavalier

The military situation in the yet young Confederacy seemed to waver between grave and hopeless in the spring of 1862. A Federal army of more than 100,000 men commanded by George B. McClellan was closing upon Richmond from the east by way of the peninsula formed by the York and James Rivers. To confront this blue host, the Confederates had a force of just over 65,000 and Robert Edward Lee. Lee had assumed command on June 1 in the wake of the Battle of Seven Pines/Fair Oaks. He immediately withdrew his army into Richmond's suburbs and set the men to work digging defensive works before the Confederate capital. However Lee had, not defensive, but offensive plans in mind. He had almost decided to try to hold Richmond with a scant force of 25,000, while the rest of his army attacked the Union right flank. To seal the trap he planned to bring Stonewall Jackson's Valley Army down from the Shenandoah and into the Federal rear. It was a bold and daring design, and success seemed to depend upon troop dispositions on the Union right. Lee had to know how strong his enemy was at the projected point of attack.

Consequently on June 10 Lee sent for Stuart and instructed him to prepare for a careful reconnaissance of the country north and east of Richmond. Next day Lee put his instructions in writing, and his orders revealed that Lee knew Stuart's mind pretty well. He gave Stuart wide discretion, but counseled him, "not to hazzard your command or to attempt what your judgment may not approve; but be content to accomplish all the good you can, without feeling it necessary to obtain all that might be desired."

By the time Stuart read his orders on June 11, he was already well into preparations for his expedition. He had selected 1200 of his troopers, plus a section of his artillery (two guns). And he had probably given some thought to matching wits, if not sabers, with his father-in-law.

As a young lieutenant, very fresh out of West Point, Stuart had served in Kansas under Colonel Philip St. George Cooke. After a whirlwind courtship Stuart married Cooke's daughter Flora in 1855. Although separated by subsequent assignments, the Stuarts honored Cooke by naming their first son Philip St. George Cooke Stuart. Then came the secession crisis. Stuart embraced the Southern Confederacy, and most of the family expected Cooke to do likewise. From Harper's Ferry, his first assignment in the Confederate army, Stuart wrote his wife, "How I hope your Pa will resign. . . . He is wanted here very much. He is highly complimented everywhere. . . . Why don't he come?" Cooke never did come. He remained in the United States Army, to the intense mortification of his son-in-law.

Once Stuart was certain that Cooke's decision was final, he proclaimed, "He will regret it but once, and that will be continually." To Flora he wrote that she should bear the shame associated with her father's action and "be consoled. . . by the reflection that your husband and brothers will atone for the father's conduct." And in a cold fury Stuart informed Flora that their son's name would be changed. He offered her several choices of names, but insisted that she never again refer to anyone called Philip St. George Cooke Stuart.

During the fall of 1861 both Cooke and Stuart received promotions to brigadier-general and important cavalry commands in rival armies. In June of 1862 Cooke commanded a division of cavalry in McClellan's army—cavalry that Stuart might logically anticipate encountering when he scouted the right flank of the Union army.

At two o'clock on the morning of June 12, Stuart roused his staff, "Gentlemen, in ten minutes every man must be in his saddle!" The statement was classic. Stuart was quite conscious of the impression he made upon others and quite careful to cultivate his own mythology. As Heros von Borcke, Prussian soldier-of-fortune and member of Stuart's military family, observed, "He delighted in the neighing of the charger and the clangor of the bugle, and he had something of Marat's weakness for the vanities of military parade. He betrayed this latter quality in his jaunty uniform, which consisted of a small grey jacket, trousers of the same stuff, and over them high military boots, a yellow silk sash, and a grey slouch hat surmounted by a sweeping black ostrich plume." Significantly, Stuart wore his jingling spurs even when he danced. And on that

Riding with a Calculating Cavalier

June morning in 1862, Stuart was a general officer only eight years out of West Point, eager to serve his new country, to prove that he was not some fortunate fop, and to raise considerable hell in the process.

In far more mundane attire and considerably later than 2 A.M., I mounted an internal combustion engine to follow Stuart's trail. I used some mimeographed directions and a map prepared by the Richmond Civil War Round Table to retrace his route. The starting point at U.S. Route 1 and Azalea Avenue was in 1862 well outside of Richmond, between the outer and intermediate lines of fortifications, hastily erected to defend the city. When I reached that intersection in 1982, I realized that Stuart's horsemen would now have very little trouble complying with their leader's order to pack three days' cooked rations. Within sight of the crossroads were White Tower Hamburgers, Hardee's, Burger King, Arby's Roast Beef, Waffle House, Del Taco, Wright's Town House ("Chicken in the Rough"), and La Casita Homemade Mexican Foods. And if these establishments were insufficient, a large shopping mall promised more "fast foods" for tardy troopers.

For almost three miles Stuart followed the modern-day Route 1 north out of Richmond. Then he turned left in order to feign a march westward, perhaps to join Jackson in the Shenandoah Valley. At this point only Stuart knew his mission, and his feint fooled his own men who sagely informed each other that they were headed for the Valley. The march on June 12 was essentially uneventful, and the Confederates camped that night on a farm about twenty-two miles from their starting point.

Characteristically, Stuart did not remain in camp; he rarely did. Whatever else the man was, he was restless and seemingly tireless. A number of Stuart's staff officers wrote memoirs about their service with him, and predictably they praised him lavishly and portrayed him as the jolliest of cavaliers. Yet none of his staff wrote much more than variations of degree and detail on these themes, and none of them seemed to know any more about Stuart than he wanted them to know. Certainly he kept his own counsel as have many leaders, military and otherwise.

But he also developed the habit of withdrawing—visiting the headquarters of other generals or calling upon households where there were charming women. And on these visits and calls he took some members of his military family, but rarely the same members over an extended period. One of Stuart's aides made a revealing comment in a letter to his sister, "It was dreadfully lonesome here all day and I wished very much that I was with the General as I have found that I am always happier when with him than anywhere else in this life we are now leading." Stuart seemed to need attention, and he carefully cultivated his image as dashing knight. Yet he seemed never to allow even those closest to him to come too close for too long.

On the night of June 12-13, he rode out of his camp to an estate called Hickory Hill. He went to visit Captain Williams C. Wickham, one of his officers who was recuperating from a battle wound. I also visited Hickory Hill and saw the room where Stuart came to wish Wickham a speedy recovery. The place remains in the Wickham family and Captain Wickham's grandson, who is a retired naval captain, at age 94, presides over the imposing house and grounds as well as 5,000 acres of fine farmland. Stories conflict about what Stuart did at Hickory Hill beside calling upon his injured comrade. One account has Stuart dozing in a chair during the evening; another has him eating breakfast with the Wickham family. The current Captain Wickham insists that Stuart did neither, "He didn't stay long enough. He just spent a few minutes with grandfather and left." Once more I had found an instance in which Stuart was everywhere and nowhere. Maybe his elusiveness was part of the fascination.

Very early on June 13, 1862, Stuart had flares sent up to signal the resumption of the march. Bugles would have attracted more attention to what was still a mysterious expedition. Soon after the column formed, however, Stuart took his subordinate officers aside and informed them of their mission. And from this point the route of march bent east and south around the flank of the Federal army. The Southern horsemen followed for some time what is now a dirt and gravel road, and it was easier for me to imagine myself within the column of troopers, even though I rode atop many more internal combustion "horses" than did whole squadrons of Confederate cavalry. The surroundings were rural, as indeed they had been ever since I left Route 1; large cedar trees lined the road; and there were woods to the right and open fields on the left. Surely, I said to myself, this place must appear much as it did in 1862. Then I looked more closely and realized that no road grader visited the area in 1862, that the woods had been cut-over within the past couple of years, and then I had to quit looking around, and search for a spot to pull over in order to avoid a very large liquid fertilizer truck that was approaching. So much for imagination.

At Hanover Court House about nine o'clock on the morning of the thirteenth, Stuart's cavalry first encountered their enemies, a small group of Federal cavalry posted in the village. When he sighted the Federals, Stuart sent Fitz Lee (Robert E. Lee's nephew) and his regiment to try to cut them off and so to prevent word of his presence and numbers from spreading. The Yankees, however, were too rapid in their withdrawal, and the Confederate's first brush with Unionists produced no bloodshed. It seemed appropriate that when I drove through Hanover Court House a local dinner-theater was playing *Much Ado About Nothing*.

From Hanover Court House the column could expect combat at any time, and the scouts Stuart sent forward reported Federal cavalry in increasing numbers observing his passage. The Confederates approached the bridge over Totopotomy Creek especially warily. A determined stand here by a force even a third the size of Stuart's might stop the Southerners or produce a delay in the march which would prove fatal to their mission. Consequently, when the Federals merely watched the Confederates from a distance while they crossed the bridge, Stuart realized that his enemy was either small, or stupid, or both.

Just about a mile from the Totopotomy, near a place called Linney's Corner, the Federals made a stand. Woods lined the road on both sides and so confined the battleground. Approximately one hundred Union cavalrymen formed in the road with no apparent intention to give ground. Immediately, Stuart passed the order, "Form fours, draw sabers, charge!"

Southern horsemen, four abreast, spurred up the road, yelling and waving their sabers. In the lead was 29-year-old Captain William Latané commanding the Essex Light Dragoons. Before this war he had practiced medicine and managed his prosperous family plantation in the Virginia Tidewater. Now he was screaming "On to them boys!" and riding his half-Arabian horse "The Colonel" about fifteen yards ahead of his men, straight at the commander of the Federal cavalry Captain William Royall. Latané closed with his enemy and slashed him with his saber. Royall was severely wounded; but he answered Latané's saber with two pistol shots. The young physician tumbled from his horse and was dead by the time he struck the roadbed.

Elsewhere the clash of mounted troops had become a "fox chase"; the Confederates scattered their foes and pressed forward. In the wake of the conflict about a half-dozen of Latané's comrades gathered around his body. Sergeant S. W. Mitchell from the company mounted his horse, and the dead man's younger brother John helped lift the corpse and drape it in front of Mitchell. Then Mitchell and John Latané left the column which had reformed to resume the march. Soon they encountered an ox-drawn cart which they commandeered as a makeshift hearse. The living Latané dismissed Mitchell, gave up his horse, and followed the ox-cart on foot to a nearby plantation called Westwood.

Because this region was "enemy country," the only white people in the vicinity were women and girls. Mrs. Catherine Brockenbrough of Westwood and Mrs. Willoughby Newton of nearby Summer Hill promised John Latané that they would give his brother a proper funeral. They gave him a horse and sent him off to rejoin Stuart. Then they began trying to carry out their promise. Nineteenth-century women were accustomed to preparing bodies for burial, and slaves were on hand to construct a coffin and dig the grave. But the women were unable to locate a clergyman to perform the burial service. So Mrs. Newton took charge and read the service at the family graveyard at Summer Hill while women and children from the neighborhood looked on.

A poignant scene it must have been. It became a scene familiar to an entire generation of Southerners. About two weeks after the burial, a woman, probably Latané's fiancée Martha Davis, wrote a letter to John R. Thompson who was a poet and former editor of the *Southern Literary Messenger* (once edited by Edgar Allan Poe). She requested Thompson to compose a poem to commemorate Latané, and Thompson responded with "The Burial of Latané." The work is a trifle maudlin, but not mawkish, and Tennyson pronounced it the "most classical poem written on either side during the war." The first and last stanzas read:

The combat raged not long, but ours the day;
   And through the hosts that compassed us around
Our little band rode proudly on its way,
   Leaving one gallant comrade, gray-crowned,
Unburied on the field he died to gain,
   Single of all his men amid the hostile slain.

And when Virginia, leaning on her spear,
Victrix et Vidua—the conflict done—
   Shall raise her mailed hand to wipe the tear
That starts, as she recalls each martyred son,
   No prouder memory her breast shall sway
Than thine, our early lost, Latané.

The *Southern Literary Messenger* published Thompson's poem in the summer of 1862, and it became an instant classic. Two years later Latané's interment again evoked artistic response. William D. Washington, a painter who specialized in historical subjects as well as portraits, set up a studio in Richmond to depict the burial of Latané on canvas. Using members of a local literary circle and some of the city's leading society maids and matrons as models, Washington worked on the painting for several months. When completed, Washington's *The Burial of Latané* drew "throngs of visitors" to its display. And soon prints of the work spread throughout the South. When the Lost Cause was indeed lost, the painting became downright sacred, a symbol of sacrifice and devotion to the Cause, and copies hung in innumerable Southern parlors during the late nineteenth century. William D. Washington's name is hardly a "household word" now. His name is buried (no pun intended) with other forgotten artists in surveys of American painting in paragraphs about "sentimentalism" and "exaggeration" characteristic of works of "historical anecdote." One such survey concludes with the patronizing judgment, "These men had their reward in their generation and their work has not survived it, except as period pieces." However condescending, the judgment is valid. And it applies to John R. Thompson's poetry, as well as to Washington's painting.

But it was "their generation," that romantic era, which concerned me. In his official report of this raid, Stuart did not simply state that Latané had died. No, Stuart reported that "the gallant captain...sealed his devotion to his native soil with his blood." Nothing would do, but that I take my cynical self on a search for Latané's grave.

Linney's Corner where the fight occurred is no longer enclosed by woods; now a subdivision stands on an all but bald hill where Latané charged and died. My sheet of directions discouraged a search for his once-famous grave, "The graveyard is quite difficult to find and cannot be reached except in dry weather." That sounded like a dare; I went in search of Summer Hill.

I became lost only once before I located the place, still in possession of the Newton family. A newspaper still in the tube indicated that no one was home, and some No Trespassing signs were less than encouraging. Nevertheless, I trespassed—parked the car, walked around a barn, said hello to some Angus heifers, headed down a farm road, then across a plowed field, and there on a rise in a grove of trees was the site. The precise location of Latané's grave is unknown; but during the 1920's the Battlefield Markers Association made a guess and erected a marker the

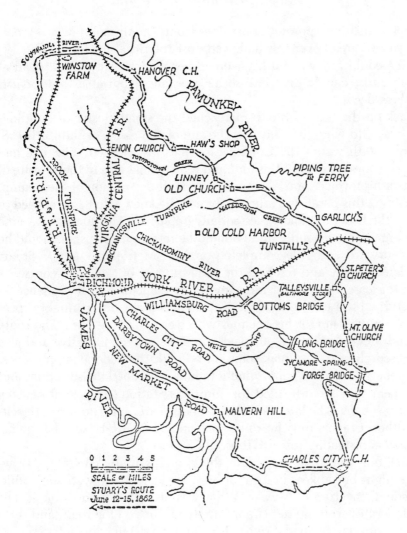

Stuart's "Ride Around McClellan." Courtesy of the Richmond Civil War Round Table.

text of which incorporated some lines from Thompson's poem, "Woman's voice...read over this hallowed dust the ritual for the dead."

All I could feel was futility—one saber against two pistols, dead at twenty-nine, cult figure because he was killed, burial as *objet d'art*, death as decor.

Back on the trail of Stuart, I reached the small cluster of buildings that was Old Church. This was the site of the camp of the Fifth U.S. Cavalry with whom the Confederates had just clashed. Fitz Lee had once served with men of this unit and took special glee in the capture of some of his former comrades and in the swift destruction of their camp. For Stuart this point was crucial. By now he knew what Lee needed to know; the Federal flank was essentially untended. The question became how to return to friendly lines: Should he retrace his steps, or should he press forward and ride completely around McClellan's army? Stuart pondered briefly and resolved the issue in favor of the latter course.

In this case his taste for fame and glory coincided with prudence. If he returned to Lee's lines by the way he had come, Stuart might expect to collide with any of his enemies who were pursuing him. The route around McClellan's army allowed him to retain the initiative and also promised chances to wreak some havoc with the Federal supply lines. The general called his subordinates to him, explained the situation, and told them they were headed for Tunstall's Station, deeper into enemy country. Then, as he later reported, "Taking care...to inquire of the citizens the distance and the route to Hanover Court House, I kept my horse's head steadily toward Tunstall's Station."

Jeb Stuart must have had many things on his mind as he rode. Always there might be Yankees in front of him. He knew there were some units of Federal cavalry in his wake. What was his father-in-law doing? The Confederates encountered Union supply wagons on the road, and these they captured or burned. Stuart also sent out a detail to burn two supply ships at a place called Putney's Ferry on the Pamunkey River. But all this capturing and burning took time. Stuart was confident that his force was sufficient to overwhelm enemy cavalry; infantry was a very different matter. If General Cooke or anyone else were able to intercept or overtake the raiders with some strong combination of horse and foot soldiers, the whole venture might become a disaster. Stuart also had to identify men in his column who were familiar with the region and make them his guides. As it happened he had selected units to participate in this raid with this requirement in mind. From Old Church to Tunstall's Station Private Richard E. Frayser was chief guide; beyond Tunstall's Station Stuart would depend upon Lieutenant Jones Christian. The questions, contingencies, and plans that must have whirled inside his head remained inside; outside, Stuart sang and joked seemingly without care: "If you want to have a good time, / Jine the cavalry. . . ."

As lead elements of the column neared Tunstall's Station vigilance increased. This place was on the tracks of the Richmond and York River Railroad, now used by McClellan as his major supply line between White House landing on the Pamunkey and the army in Richmond's suburbs. Then at the worst of times, one of Stuart's two artillery pieces became stuck in a mudhole. The men thrashed the horses, and the lieutenant in charge shouted encouragement; but the gun would not move. Then a sergeant called the lieutenant aside and made a brief suggestion. The lieutenant nodded and ordered a small barrel of whiskey recently liberated from a Union supply wagon placed on the gun. He promised the contents of the barrel to the gunners when the gun was again mobile. Instantly the men waded into the mudhole, wrenched the gun out, and fell to lapping up their reward.

Unfortunately for Stuart, the combination of mud and whiskey detained his artillery too long. The horsemen swept into Tunstall's and quickly suppressed two companies of Federals stationed there. But as the Southerners began cutting telegraph wires and trying to tear up railroad track, they heard a rumble and a whistle. A train was coming from the direction of Richmond. The men erected a crude barricade on the tracks and waited. Very soon the train appeared. When the engineer saw the barricade he increased his speed and ran through the obstruction. Seeing this, Captain Will Farley grabbed a shotgun and spurred his horse in pursuit of the engine. Farley rode alongside the engine and blasted the unfortunate engineer just as he believed he had made good his escape. Those aboard who survived the gauntlet of Rebel fire did escape, thanks to the bold engineer who did not. Without artillery, Stuart's cavalry could not stop the speeding train.

Will Farley lived just less than one year longer than the engineer he killed. On June 9, 1863, the young captain who served as one of Stuart's volunteer scouts had his leg blown off by an artillery shell. As he was carried to an ambulance he pointed to his severed leg on the ground and asked to have it. "It's an old friend, gentlemen, and I do not wish to part with it." Farley went off to die hugging the lifeless stump. Recalling the circumstances of Farley's death and his concern for a grand gesture—even while in what must have been great pain—made it difficult for me to reconcile his almost casual bloodthirst involved in killing the Union engineer. Maybe the young man was acting out some romantic, pastoral rebellion against a machine. War is a grisly business; maybe I was thinking too much.

Tunstall's Station still has railroad tracks, but little else. The small railroad station is closed and I saw only two houses. I realized at Tunstall's how conditioned I was to growth and "progress." Many of the communities on 1862 maps have disappeared or at least declined radically since that time. I guessed that Tunstall's Station was a thriving little place as long as the Richmond and York River Railroad was of some local consequence. But when Interstate 64, among other highways, bypassed the place, it simply ceased to be a thriving little place.

Stuart left Tunstall's after dark on the night of June 13 and rode about $4^{1}/_{2}$ miles to a place called Talleysville. There Stuart stopped for $3^{1}/_{2}$ hours to allow the men some rest and to close up his straggling column. The Confederates found a Union hospital at Talleysville which they did not disturb: They also found sutlers, merchants who sold to soldiers, and their well-stocked stores. These the hungry Rebels disturbed quite a bit. A single member of Stuart's military family consumed at Talleysville figs, beef tongue, pickle, candy, tomato catsup, preserves, lemons, cakes, sausages, molasses, crackers, and canned meats. Amazingly he survived this gluttony and rode out of Talleysville when Stuart reformed his column at midnight.

At this point Stuart had to focus most of his concern upon the Chickahominy River. His troops had crossed the Chickahominy once before on this ride, before dawn on June 12. Then the river was a small creek. At this point on Stuart's route, the Chickahominy was more formidible; crossing the stream required a bridge or a ford. Stuart's guide for this portion of the march Lieutenant Jones Christian knew of a ford; in fact, the ford was on property belonging to Christian's family. However, when the leading elements of the Southern column reached the ford at dawn, they discovered the river very high.

Colonel W. H. F. ("Rooney") Lee, second son of the commanding general, plunged into the swirling water and with difficulty swam to the far bank. Lee pronounced the ford definitely unfordable and, again in danger of drowning, swam back. Next the troopers tried to fell trees across the stream in order to construct a bridge. However, the trees were slightly short and as they crashed into the river, the current swept them downstream. At this juncture Stuart arrived on the scene and stroked his beard thoughtfully while he listened to reports of what had been done. About a mile downstream were the ruins of a bridge, and Stuart decided to have a try at rebuilding the structure.

The men worked as rapidly as possible using boards from a nearby warehouse to repair the span. Meanwhile Stuart set out one of his regiments as a rear guard. The situation was a bit tense as morning wore on. Federal cavalry in small numbers challenged the rear guard and were fairly easily repulsed. But no one knew when the enemy might arrive in strength and trap the raiders. As it happened the Federals never did appear in numbers large enough to threaten. By about one o'clock the bridge was complete, the Confederates across, and the bridge burned.

Stuart led his weary band to Charles City Court House, about 7 miles from the Chickahominy, and called a halt to permit men and horses to rest. At sunset the general with two companions left his command and pressed on toward Richmond about 28 miles away. He stopped only once for coffee, arrived before sunrise on June 15, and went at once to Lee's headquarters. The rest of his men rode into Richmond later the same day.

The Chickahominy was fairly high from recent rains when I saw it. I scrambled through some briars to the bank, but decided against trying to swim across as Rooney Lee had done. Full colonels in command of regiments do not normally now dive into rivers to determine how safe is the passage. Neither do historians. The bridge was stable and cars roared across with none of the difficulty that beset Stuart and his men. From Charles City Court House, where Stuart rested briefly and then left his men to hurry ahead to Lee, his route is now Route 5 parallel to the James River. The road is designated a "Virginia ByWay," and indeed it was when I traveled it—lots of woods and large farms. Route 5 emphasized what I had noticed throughout my sojourn on Stuart's trail. Here I was, never more than about 30 miles from Richmond, and the countryside was overwhelmingly rural. On large maps of the United States showing population density, this entire area is shaded in the color denoting most people per square mile. On maps depicting industrial development, a brown circle standing for "manufacturing center" coincides almost precisely with the land area enclosed by Stuart's circuit around McClellan. Geographers and others are fond of projecting an east coast megalopolis extending now from Boston to Richmond and within the next few decades from Boston to Atlanta. Yet here was I, in the midst of brown circles and megalopolis, and all I saw was green farmland, woodland, and a very few subdivisions. I saw no "fast food" franchises, only a couple of convenience stores, and many more country general stores than supermarkets. Not everything was pretty. There were asbestos-sided shacks and some recently cut timberland that looked like the Battle of Verdun had happened yesterday. Yet on the whole, I was heartened that this history happened in such a nice place.

Richmond happened suddenly. I crested a hill on Route 5, and there was a skyline much different from the one Stuart saw in 1862. Very soon I was stuck in traffic on Main Street staring at tall buildings recently built and being built. I had completed Stuart's "ride"; it was time to think about what the expedition meant and to ponder some answers to my questions about Jeb Stuart.

In 1862 Stuart's "ride around McClellan," or "Pamunkey expedition," or "Chickahominy raid" as it was variously called, was an enormous success. Not only was Stuart able to tell Lee what he needed to know, that the Federal flank was vulnerable, and thus enable Lee to conduct what became the Seven Days Campaign that drove the Union army away from Richmond and thwarted McClellan's threat to the Confederate Capital. Stuart also inflicted some damage upon the Union supply line, and he fed McClellan's fears that he, not Lee, was in grave danger. Stuart did wonders for Southern morale at a time when the war seemed to be going quite badly. Lee published a general order announcing "great satisfaction" at the "brilliant exploit." Virginia Governor John Letcher presented Stuart with a ceremonial saber. Newspapers throughout the Confederacy were lavish in their praise, and Stuart was the toast of the capital.

He did not meet his father-in-law in battle; but that was not Stuart's fault. Philip St. George Cooke spent many frustrating hours during his son-in-law's caper. He received reports that Stuart had many more cavalry troops than he actually had and that the Rebels had five regiments of infantry (5,000 men!) as well. Cooke believed these reports and pursued Stuart cautiously. He collected cavalry units and secured infantry support. Philip St. George Cooke was a prudent person; he died in bed at age eighty-three. His audacious son-in-law fell mortally wounded on a battlefield at age thirty-one.

But what about Stuart alive? What had I learned about him during this circuit? One of Stuart's staff later reminded him of the tense time they had had trying to cross the Chickahominy:

"That was a tight place at the river General. If the enemy had come down on us you would have been compelled to surrender."

"No," was his reply; "one other course was left."

"What was that?"

"To die game."

Stuart was indeed a romantic hero. But he was more besides. He was a self-made myth, a calculating cavalier. All the while he was riding through the countryside joking and singing "jine the cavalry," Stuart was measuring odds in his mind and anticipating many miles ahead. He was carefree, not careless. Maybe the key to Stuart was balance. He wore his plume; he was a consummate professional. But his profession was war, and he chose to live "on the outer limits of probability." His ride around McClellan was a *quest*, a *mission*, a *lark*. Stuart harmonized this trinity in himself and acted out the blend.

Once I completed retracing Stuart's route I could put away my sheet of directions and relax a bit. I pressed a cassette tape of unknown substance into a player and punched the "play" button. The tape contained a very strange mixture of music—Vivaldi's *The Four Seasons*, and some very recent rock songs. These sounds, invading the same set of ears in succession, had to constitute the penultimate counterpoint—baroque and rock, "barock"? I was still thinking about Stuart, still trying to reconcile the concepts of quest, mission, and lark. And among the seemingly dissonant elements of the sounds and the thoughts, there was a strange consonance.

TOTAL WAR AND APRICOT JAM

When Americans go to war, they usually fight in someone else's country. Soldiers go into combat "overseas," and later join the Veterans of Foreign Wars. The vast majority of Americans come no closer to a war zone during wartime than the atlases they consult to find out where in the world are such places as Palermo, Peleliu, Pusan, and Pleiku. To be sure, British redcoats marched about North America during the Revolution and even sacked Washington during the War of 1812. But British armies were never very large in those days, and relatively speaking the damage they did was slight and of short duration.

The great exception to this American rule of wars was of course the Civil War. And with few exceptions, the war zones of that conflict lay in the American South. The American Civil War also marked a significant step in evolution of "total war"—war between peoples, instead of being restricted to armies. Consequently Southern civilians were some of the first of the world's peoples to endure the dangers and devastation of campaigns waged directly against morale and economic resources.

"Morale and economic resources" are abstract terms. In Southern memory, the advent of "total war" usually evokes more concrete manifestations. Let me offer a personal example.

Located about twenty miles east of Richmond in King William County, Virginia, is "Chestnut Grove" where six generations of one branch of my family have lived. The house is old—built in the eighteenth century—but unpretentious. It is definitely a "homeplace" as opposed to an "ancestral seat."

During the "late unpleasantness" Union cavalry frequently raided the countryside around Chestnut Grove—so much so that the family had a prescribed drill through which they went whenever the Yankees came near. My great-grandfather Andrew Macon Pollard, who was a boy then, had the task of driving the livestock away from the house and into a swamp so the Federals would not find them. After some false alarms, one day the Yankee raiders came in earnest, and when Andrew returned to the house from his errand, he learned that the enemy had broken into the smokehouse. The Yankees had taken as much meat as they could carry and more than they could eat. As they rode away, the blue-coated horsemen hacked off hunks of ham and bacon with the sabers and dropped the meat in the dusty road. No doubt they considered this tactic a legitimate act of war, because they were depriving their enemy of food.

My great-great-grandmother had a very different opinion. Moreover she determined to salvage as much of the cured meat as possible. Accordingly she dispatched young Andrew to follow the raiders. The boy ran after the Yankee column, and as he ran he retrieved chunks of meat from the dirt. He returned them to the farm where his mother washed and returned them to the smokehouse.

Needless to say this incident has been told and retold in my family, and the Yankees involved seldom got much credit for their zeal in conducting "total war." One of the recent times I heard the story occurred during a sojourn on the trail of Ulric Dahlgren.

Although his name is not a household word in the national memory, Ulric Dahlgren acquired some local fame—or infame—in and around Richmond during early 1864. He led a party of Federal horsemen on a daring raid against the Confederate capital. In the process he began a controversy about the morality of "total war" that raged long after Appomattox and indeed sputters still.

Son of a distinguished Union admiral, John A. Dahlgren, "Ully" had grown up in Washington, D.C. The outbreak of the Civil War interrupted young Dahlgren's legal studies in a Philadelphia law office; he volunteered for the army to avoid the stigma of favoritism from his father, the prominent naval officer. Commissioned a captain, Dahlgren served on several staffs and in the course of his duties commanded small units of Federal cavalry in combat. In the wake of the fighting at Gettysburg, he suffered a bullet wound in his foot at Boonsboro, Pennsylvania, but remained in action with his command until he passed out from loss of blood.

Dahlgren's gallantry earned him a promotion to colonel, but may have contributed to the loss of his leg. His wound did not heal properly, and surgeons had to amputate the leg below the knee. Supported by a wooden peg, the young (23) colonel journeyed to the Federal fleet blockading Charleston to convalesce aboard his father's ship. Dahlgren returned to Washington in late January, 1864, soon after he heard rumors of an impending raid on Richmond and was determined to take part.

The raid began in the mind of Federal cavalry General Hugh Judson Kilpatrick who seemed ever in search of conspicuous heroics. Probably through influential political friends, Kilpatrick gained an interview with Abraham Lincoln on the president's birthday and proposed a new coup.

According to Elizabeth Van Lew who operated a small but well-organized network of Unionist sympathizers in Richmond, the Confederate capital was only lightly defended and ripe for the taking. Called "Crazy Bet" behind her back by unsuspecting neighbors, Van Lew used her eccentric habits and demeanor as a cover for espionage activities that produced reliable intelligence. If she said Richmond could be had, it probably could. And once inside the city Federal raiders would have allies more formidable than Van Lew's small band of spies. Large numbers of Union prisoners of war, perhaps as many as 10,000, were in Richmond, and if Kilpatrick could free them, the potential for mayhem was enormous. Kilpatrick counted upon Lincoln's concern for the welfare of the Federal prisoners who endured their confinement in circumstances far less than ideal. He knew, too, that Lincoln wanted some means of distributing copies of an amnesty proclamation by which he offered full pardons to Confederates who renewed their allegiance to the United

States. The cavalry general emphasized Richmond's vulnerability, the plight of Union prisoners, and the opportunity for disseminating the president's proclamation, and Lincoln listened receptively.

Even though Kilpatrick's superiors were skeptical, Lincoln endorsed the great raid—4,000 troopers and some light artillery unleashed upon Richmond. And Dahlgren was able to secure for himself a prominent role in the venture. While Kilpatrick led 3,500 horsemen into Richmond from the north, Dahlgren commanding a detached force of 500 would dash into the city from the south.

Although Dahlgren still walked with the aid of a crutch, he assured his father he could "stand the service perfectly well without my leg." His enthusiasm for the undertaking was boundless. "If successful," he wrote, "it will be the grandest thing on record. . . . I may be captured, or I may be *'tumbled over'*; but it is an undertaking that if I were not in, I should be ashamed to show my face again."

As far as possible Kilpatrick and Dahlgren maintained strict security about the risky business they plotted. On February 26 Kilpatrick received his final orders; the raid would commence on February 28 near dark. On that Sunday evening Dahlgren led his 500 men from camp at Stevensburg and across the Rapidan River at Ely's Ford. Kilpatrick followed with the larger column. The raiders rode all night, and then about daybreak on February 29 at Spotsylvania Court House, Dahlgren turned off the route Kilpatrick would take and headed for Goochland Court House, a little village near the James River about thirty miles above Richmond.

The weather turned miserable on February 29, 1864, and both bands of Federals rode through cold rain and sleet. Although they had broken through Robert E. Lee's Confederate army guarding the Rapidan, the raiders could hardly expect to continue unchallenged. But they met little resistance en route; and as it happened, Elizabeth Van Lew was correct, Richmond was quite lightly defended. Kilpatrick reached the intermediate defense lines of the city around midday on March 1, and then, unaccountably, lost his nerve.

Total War and Apricot Jam

On the verge of attacking the 500 or so Southerners who stood between him and his prize, Kilpatrick called off his assault and withdrew. He led his raiders eventually to the safety of Federal lines down the Virginia Peninsula. There were circumstances that mitigated Kilpatrick's failure: his men were exhausted from 43 hours of constant riding, the weather had taken its toll, and Kilpatrick could not know for sure the weakness of his enemy. Yet even when these factors, and more which Kilpatrick made up, are counted, his performance appears poor.

Of course Kilpatrick adroitly tried to explain away his failure in his report of the expedition. But the main reason he escaped large amounts of blame for his lost opportunity had little to do with anything he did or said. Very soon after Kilpatrick's men made their way to safety, the army, press, and public forgot them. The central figure in the aborted raid became not Kilpatrick, but Dahlgren.

The young colonel rode hard all day on February 29 and pressed on into the darkness on the road to Goochland Court House. Finally at about two o'clock on the morning of March 1, Dahlgren called a halt, and the Federals made camp about nine miles from Goochland Court House.

Before full light on March 1 Dahlgren was again in the saddle. The weather was still foreboding, but at least the raiders could see the road and each other. Early in the morning the column reached the James and the James River and Kanawa Canal which ran parallel to the river. Dahlgren was still 21 miles from Richmond and needed to quicken his pace if he were to cross the James and strike the city from the south in some concert with Kilpatrick. Accordingly the Colonel divided his force and sent Captain John F. B. Mitchell with 100 men, directly toward Richmond along the canal. En route Mitchell's force was to destroy mills and canal locks, tasks which would only slow down the main column. Meanwhile Dahlgren would press on down the River Road, cross the James, and complete his course to Richmond.

Dahlgren dashed off with his 400 troopers to find a ford across the James. He had no concern about locating the crossing, because he had brought with him from Stevensburg a guide who supposedly knew the area well. The guide was Martin Robinson, a free black bricklayer, sent to Dahlgren from the Provost-Marshal General's office in Washington. Robinson had once been a slave; he had lived near Goochland Court House and knew well the location of Jude's Ferry where the raiders intended to cross the James. Dahlgren had struck a bargain with Robinson. The black man would lead the raiders to the ford, and once they were across Robinson would be free to leave and considerably richer. If, however, the bricklayer failed or played his employers false, he would be hanged on the spot.

Robinson dutifully conducted Dahlgren's column to Jude's Ferry and halted on the river bank where he remembered the ford to be. But as the guide and the raiders stared down at the water it was instantly evident that they could not cross there. The brown water swirled below and beyond the normal bed of the river. There was a steam ferry at Jude's Ferry, but it was moored unattended on the opposite shore. In truth there was normally a ford there, but the torrential rains of the past several days had swollen the river and erased all traces of the crossing. Unfortunately for Robinson his agreement made no allowance for extenuating circumstances, and Dahlgren was in no mood to amend the bargain. The Federal commander immediately concluded that Martin Robinson had betrayed him and would have to suffer the consequences. Robinson realized his predicament and allowed himself to be led to a roadside tree with no protest. There he was hanged with his own bridle reins.

I admit I had no more luck finding Jude's Ferry ford than did Martin Robinson. I did intersect Dahlgren's raid route at several points. At Stevensburg, where the expedition began, I found a crossroads farming community probably no larger now than in 1864. At Ely's Ford on the Rapidan, I found a bridge there now. I went to Goochland and from there retraced Dahlgren's route toward Richmond. But I could not decide whether or not the bridge that now spans the James on Route 522 marks the site of Jude's Ferry. Perhaps I should have looked more thoroughly. I am sure I would have, had someone been threatening to strangle me with my seat-belt strap.

Dahlgren left Martin Robinson's lifeless body dangling from a tree limb and pressed on down the River Road toward Richmond. He knew that he would have to abandon his plan to enter Richmond from the south, and so he decided to continue his present course and strike from the west. Dahlgren's men stopped briefly at some of the handsome estates that bordered the James, burned some barns, and collected some booty.

At Sabot Hill, the plantation home of Confederate Secretary of War James A. Seddon, Dahlgren led his troopers into the yard, dismounted, with the aid of his crutch stumped up the steps to the front door, and knocked. When the door opened Dahlgren sent for the lady of the house and introduced himself. Sallie Bruce Seddon remembered the Colonel as little "Ully," and in fact Dahlgren's father had once been one of her beaus. She invited the enemy raider inside and sent for some 20-year-old blackberry wine. Then the pair sat down, toasted each other, and talked of old times. Mrs. Seddon's hospitality toward "Ully" grown up was perhaps genuine; but she had other plans for Dahlgren the Yankee raider. While she entertained her guest, a rider from Sabot Hill spurred away toward Richmond to give the alarm.

Concluding the bizarre interlude in his raid, Dahlgren assured his hostess that her home would not be harmed and took his leave. Other residents of the neighborhood were not so fortunate. Mitchell's troopers, for example, tried three times to burn the home of James M. Morson at "Dover." Morson's slaves insisted upon putting out the fires; so the Federals satisfied themselves with quenching their thirsts with Morson's vintage wine and taking silver goblets with them in which to finish their drinks. At 3:30 P.M., Mitchell's detachment, leaving a trail of destruction and burning behind it, overtook Dahlgren's main body at Short Pump, a crossroads about eight miles from Richmond. There the raiders rested and fed themselves and their horses. The skies, which had been leaden and drippy all day, opened again, and rain mixed with sleet began falling steadily.

At about five o'clock Dahlgren first heard the guns involved in Kilpatrick's encounter with Richmond's defenses. The colonel quickly formed his column and began his final approach to the capital. The Federals advanced down the Three Chopt Road to Westham and then took the Westham Plank Road toward the city. They rode about three miles from Short Pump without incident. Then about five miles from Richmond sharpshooters began firing into the horsemen from the sides of the road. In the growing darkness the raiders found it impossible to detect their enemy save by the flash of their weapons. The Southerners were members of home guard units—surely they were scared and confused; but so must have been the Federal horsemen as they entered an enemy city amid rain, sleet, and dark.

At last the firing from the roadside became fairly general, and Dahlgren determined to ride down his tormentors. He ordered a series of charges each time the firing increased, and horse soldiers pressed on to the forks of Cary Street. There on the outskirts of the city the amalgam of citizen soldiers stood their ground. After a final, futile charge, Dahlgren passed the word to withdraw. In the dark confusion Dahlgren and about 100 of his men became separated from the rest of the force. Eventually most of the raiders were able to find Kilpatrick and ride with him to safety. Dahlgren and his contingent were not so fortunate.

I followed Dahlgren's trail into Richmond's suburbs, and then lost him in the maze of the modern city. I recovered his hoof prints later when he was scrambling toward Federal lines.

Dahlgren rode all night around Richmond, according to one witness "as fast as the men and horses could stand it." Just after daybreak, the Colonel called a halt and with his weary men ate a bit of breakfast. At this point early on the morning of March 2, Dahlgren had been riding and thinking for upwards to sixty hours with little respite in miserable weather. The recent amputee, who had seen no action since July of the previous year, was justifiably worn out. Yet Dahlgren still seemed alert. He decided to make a wide detour of Richmond and the Confederates who were pursuing Kilpatrick, to cross the Pamunkey and Mattaponi rivers, and then to head southeast toward Union lines at Gloucester Point on the north bank of the York River. This circuitous route demanded more riding but promised less chance of contact with sizable bodies of Confederates.

Accordingly, when his men and mounts had eaten and rested briefly, Dahlgren formed his column and set out for Hanovertown on the Pamunkey River. The sky was clearing finally, but the day was cold. Still early in the morning the Federals reached Hanovertown and found the Pamunkey high. There was a boat on the opposite shore, however, and two of Dahlgren's troopers had to swim the frigid river to get the boat. Horses swam while men shuttled across in the small boat. Once on the north bank and into King William County, Dahlgren struck out for the Mattaponi, the last stream of any real consequences he would have to cross to reach Gloucester Point and safety. At this point he rode quite close (within two miles) to Chestnut Grove where my ancestors lived. The network of roads changed somewhat between then and now, but I was again able to follow the Federal route.

The column of blue-coated cavalry riding in broad daylight through King William County, an area relatively untouched by the war thus far, could hardly pass unnoticed. Local residents spread the word, and the raiders noticed that they were being observed. Several troopers at the head of the party put on Confederate uniforms to cause perhaps some crucial moments of indecision should they encounter home guard units. Thus Dahlgren hoped to retain at least the element of surprise.

Already, though, local men and boys were mustering and preparing to confront the raiders. And the leader of this resistance was no aging farmer but an officer of the regular cavalry. Lieutenant James Pollard commanded Lee's Rangers, or more formally Company H, Ninth Virginia Cavalry, and he and his men were home on furlough to rest and recruit in the counties of King William and King and Queen. As soon as he heard of the enemy presence and discerned Dahlgren's route, Pollard assembled as many of his men as he could (about twenty-five). He also requested aid from home guard units and from the commanders of other furloughed troops in the vicinity.

One of the home guards units from King and Queen County was actually the student body of a small school. Edward W. Halbach taught the school and commanded the military company. Halbach's health was not good enough for him to serve in the Confederate army, but he took his home guard duties seriously and drilled his pupils faithfully. Indeed one of Halbach's protégés was in the process of securing a place in John S. Mosby's famed band of partisan rangers.

"Benny" Fleet already had a letter of introduction to Mosby from Halbach, and on February 29 Benny's father paid $1,000 for a Canadian horse for Benny to ride to war. On March 2 Benny and two companions responded to the alarm caused by the raiders and rode from their homes into King William County to scout Dahlgren's movements. Shortly after noon the three young men saw three riders approaching them on the road. The strangers wore Confederate uniforms, but looked somewhat suspicious. "Are you friends or enemies?" one of the youths called out when they were about thirty yards away. "Friends," came the response, but then the column of Federal cavalry appeared behind the strangers, and the local lads knew instantly who they were. Benny and his friends wheeled their horses and attempted to flee. The Federals fired and hit two of the three. Benny was able to make it to the woods. Benny's horse returned home without him and the next day Benny's dog Stuart led the family to his master's body. Benny was lying under a pine tree, dead from loss of blood.

Dahlgren's force met other scouts that day as they rode toward the Mattaponi, and when they reached the river at Aylett's about 1:00 P.M., a small party of Southerners fired on them from the far bank. Dahlgren, himself, stood boldly on the riverbank and exhorted his men to return the fire and drive the Rebels away. They did so, and then crossed the Mattaponi by shuttling a rowboat back and forth for the men while the horses swam. Pollard and his remnant company, meanwhile had gone to a place called Dunkirk just upriver from Aylett's in the hope of intercepting the Federals at the ferry crossing there. When he realized that Dahlgren had eluded him, Pollard dashed off in pursuit. He overtook the raiders about four o'clock in the afternoon near Bruington Church approximately eight miles from Aylett's. There Dahlgren fought a rearguard action and made his escape as night came on.

Pollard's force followed the raiders a short way; then the Confederate lieutenant assigned a few of his men to continue the chase and withdrew. A light rain was falling as Pollard led his troopers by way of a short cut through Stevensville. There he picked up Edward Halbach and one of his students, 13-year-old William Littlepage. Recruits were flocking to Pollard's band and most of them were mounted; but Halbach and Littlepage remained afoot and followed the Southerners as best they could. Pollard took his followers into an ambush at a crossroads just south of Stevensville. There the road from Stevensville intersected the River Road which ran parallel to the Mattaponi toward Gloucester Point. Pollard reasoned correctly that Dahlgren would have to pass this way, and consequently he stationed his force in the woods at the crossroads and instructed them to wait.

Dahlgren, meanwhile, rode into Stevensville and called a halt for a brief rest. The colonel dozed for a time, then reformed his column, and rode off into the darkness. He was determined to use the night to elude his pursuers and avoid further skirmishing. The raiders had just begun their trek when they reached the crossroads where Pollard's force lay in ambush. From the roadside came a shouted challenge and the Federals halted. Dahlgren himself spurred his horse and rode quickly to the head of the column. He commanded the unknown challengers to surrender. Then from out of the blackness a volley of shots exploded: The young colonel who had dreamed of glory pitched off his mount and rolled into a ditch beside the road. Five bullets had struck him, and he died almost instantly.

The leaderless raiders scattered as their enemies continued to fire.

Most of the Federals drifted into a field across the river road and from there attempted to escape on foot. In the dark, however, it was impossible to distinguish ambushers from ambushees, and most of the troops on both sides simply settled down to wait out the night.

Back at the point of ambush young William Littlepage crept out of the woods to the road. He had seen an enemy fall, and the boy wanted a pocket watch. He had none, and he knew that Yankees had previously taken a watch from Halbach his schoolmaster; thus Littlepage considered it his right to relieve the dead man's pockets, but missed the watch which was in the overcoat. He did find a cigar case, some papers, and a notebook, and he discovered that his victim had a wooden leg.

Having completed his search the boy returned to Halbach and with him settled down to spend the night in the woods. "Mr. Halbach," Littlepage inquired, "Will you have a cigar?"

The teacher declined and then thought to ask where the boy had found cigars. Littlepage replied that he had found a cigar case in the pocket of the dead Yankee with a wooden leg who lay beside the road.

Littlepage added that he had found some papers on the dead man, and offered them to Halbach. The teacher took the papers; but no one dared to make a light by which to read them. At daylight the next morning (March 3) Halbach inspected the dead Federal's effects. Then only could he be sure that the raiders would not capture him and hang him in retaliation for disturbing their leader's corpse. When morning came the Confederates were able to reassemble themselves and capture most of the scattered raiders. At this point the Kilpatrick–Dahlgren raid came to a formal end.

I traced the routes of Dahlgren and his pursuers and came finally to the ambush site. The place is peaceful now; young pines border the narrow road. The field across the river road is now a county landfill, and in places the Virginia Highway Department has altered the roadbed slightly. But it is not too difficult to find the old roadbed and there to imagine the scene on that dark March midnight in 1864 and the excitement next morning when Halbach read those captured papers. Then did Dahlgren's raid assume, for Southerners at least, an enduring infamy.

The papers and memorandum book taken off Dahlgren's body apparently included his notes about the raid taken at Stevensburg, a copy of his address to his men concerning their mission and conduct, and instructions given to Captain Mitchell who commanded Dahlgren's detached force. Most of the material was mundane; it concerned such things as the composition of the raiding party, the route to be followed, and plans for coordination between Dahlgren and Kilpatrick. Some of the notes, however, and especially portions of Dahlgren's address to his followers and orders to Mitchell genuinely shocked those who read them.

"Jeff. Davis and Cabinet must be killed on the spot."

"The men must keep together and well in hand, and once in the city it must be destroyed and Jeff. Davis and Cabinet killed."

"We hope to release the prisoners from Belle Island first, and having seen them fairly started, we will cross the James River into Richmond, destroying the bridges after us and exhorting the released prisoners to destroy and burn the hateful city; and do not allow the Rebel leader Davis and his traitorous crew to escape."

Halbach, acting in his capacity as captain of his schoolboy company of home guards, gave Dahlgren's papers and memorandum book to Lieutenant Pollard who maintained informal command of the Confederate party. Pollard in turn took the documents and Dahlgren's wooden leg to Richmond and handed them to his commander Fitzhugh Lee. Lee immediately showed the material to Jefferson Davis. The Confederate president laughed when he read aloud, "Jeff. Davis and Cabinet must be killed on the spot." He turned to his Secretary of State Judah P. Benjamin who happened to be present and remarked, "That means you, Mr. Benjamin."

Others in the Confederate governmental and military hierarchy did not share the president's good humor about the Dahlgren papers. Davis' military advisor and good friend Braxton Bragg made sure that Richmond's newspapers received a copy of the papers. And when the papers printed Dahlgren's notes and orders, Southerners responded in outrage. Newspaper editors in Richmond were unanimous in their opinion that captured raiders should be tried as murderers and arsonists and hanged. Robert E. Lee called the raid a "barbarous and inhuman plot." Varina Davis remembered, "Once Commodore Dahlgren had brought the little fair-haired boy to show me how pretty he looked in his black velvet suit and Vandyke collar. . . ." Then when she reflected upon the boy grown to manhood who had sought to kill her husband, she, "could not reconcile the two Ulrics."

Eventually, about a month after the raid, Lee wrote a formal protest to George G. Meade about Dahlgren's intentions and inquired if the raiders' instructions reflected the policy of the United States. Meade responded quickly that such was not the case; neither his government nor his command sanctioned the kind of warfare prescribed in the Dahlgren papers.

Yet even before Meade framed his reply to the South's charges of attempted atrocity, the North took its turn at outrage over the Dahlgren affair. Admiral Dahlgren naturally wanted his son's body to have a fitting burial on Northern soil. Accordingly he made first proper, then frantic, appeals through the prisoner exchange commission to have the body delivered through the lines. The Confederates at first protested that Dahlgren's remains were already decently interred. Then later the Confederate commissioner of exchange admitted with some embarrassment that no one could find Dahlgren's body. Already the admiral knew that his son's wooden leg had been removed and that some Southerner in his zeal to steal the dead Colonel's ring had cut off a finger to get it. Now the Confederates confessed that they lost what remained of young Dahlgren's remains.

This grisly comedy of errors began back in King and Queen County at the crossroads where Dahlgren died. There the captured Federal raiders requested a proper burial for their fallen leader. Halbach and others among the home guard determined to comply with the request, and the

schoolmaster himself carved a wooden headboard. The Southerners prepared a coffin and removed Dahlgren's body from its initial shallow
grave. They were just about to bury the young colonel when a message
arrived from Richmond ordering Dahlgren's body to the capital. In
Richmond the body, after having been properly identified, was interred
in an unmarked grave in Oakwood Cemetery. Jefferson Davis apparently feared that some of his fellow Confederates might vent their wrath
at Dahlgren's mission by mutilating his body further. The president
along with a few others knew where the grave was, and great was their
surprise to discover it empty when the commissioner of exchange visited
the site. Davis ordered an investigation, but the Confederates in Richmond never could locate the missing body.

Credit for this minor coup belonged to Elizabeth Van Lew. The spy
set her clandestine network in motion and with creditable speed Richmond's Unionists located Dahlgren's grave, removed the body, and spir-
ited it out of the city. Until the war's end Dahlgren's remains lay beneath
a fruit tree on a farm just outside Richmond. Finally on November 1,
1865, the well-traveled body received its final interment in Philadelphia.

By this time the Confederacy was no more. Still, however, Dahlgren
and his papers evoked controversy on both sides of Mason and Dixon's
line. Admiral Dahlgren led a host of Northerners who pronounced the
papers forgeries, crude propaganda weapons designed to swell Southern
morale and generate sympathy for the Confederacy in Europe. Chief
among the reasons to suspect forgery was Dahlgren's alleged signature
on the address to his men. The document was signed "U. Dalhgren."
The colonel customarily used his full Christian name Ulric in his signature, and surely Dahlgren knew how to spell his own last name. Southerners countered by pointing to the accuracy of the details mentioned in
the notes, the identifiable handwriting, and the integrity of those who
handled the documents before they were published. The elder Dahlgren
in 1871 wrote a book about his son's life, termed his death *"assassination,"* and the documents forgeries. Southerners replied in the *Southern*

Historical Society Papers and produced statements from all concerned to demonstrate the authenticity of the papers.

Eventually the original Dahlgren papers disappeared, and only one photographic copy of Dahlgren's alleged address to his men remains. Historian Virgil Carrington Jones after exhaustive research in the preparation of his monograph about the raid, *Eight Hours Before Richmond*, concluded that the papers were genuine. After publication of his book Jones pursued the matter even further. Using photographic equipment at the National Archives Jones satisfied himself that the misspelling in Dahlgren's signature resulted from ink soaking through the paper from the reverse side and creating the appearance of the "l" and "h" transposition.

However, even if the Dahlgren papers were genuine, no one can prove that the young colonel ever delivered the address exhorting his troops to burn Richmond and kill Confederate civil officials. If he did not, then Dahlgren never translated his intentions into orders and thus actions. Hence the mystery remains.

The furor over the authenticity of Dahlgren's papers and designs serves now to obscure a point much more significant. The exchange of outrage, charges, and countercharges over the Dahlgren raid are important in and of themselves. They are a vivid commentary upon values and standards that now seem unreal.

In this "enlightened" present, the destruction of an enemy capital and the killing of enemy political leaders have become accepted methods of warfare. After all, we destroy villages to save them, sanction many forms of mass murder in the conduct of war, and elevate our standards of conduct only slightly in time of peace. The fact that participants on both sides of the American Civil War abhorred such tactics is some measure of their innocence of the consequences of "total" war.

I thought about this irony on the way back to Chestnut Grove and suppertime. Then I remembered another March visit of the Yankee army to my family's home.

The second visit to Chestnut Grove by elements of the U.S. Army occurred in March of 1978 as part of a training exercise conducted by two battalions of the 82nd Airborne Division. About 1,000 airborne troopers in maroon berets shouldering 60-pound packs trudged past the farm near the end of a 33-mile forced march. Led by a full colonel who wore his military academy ring where some people wear a wedding band, the soldiers were intense and impressive. During the exercise they covered almost 100 miles in three days, a performance which ranks with that of Stonewall Jackson's "foot cavalry."

Although the comments of some troopers regarding the march may have offended a few genteel ears among those who stood on the roadside to watch the procession, these "Yankees" were quite well-behaved. Not only did they stay away from the smokehouse at Chestnut Grove, they even left some food to replace that which their predecessors had carried off more than a century ago. After the troops had passed, my father found by the side of the road a very small, olive drab tin can. If the label is accurate, the can contains: "JAM [comma] APRICOT, Kern Foods, Inc.; Los Angeles, Calif. 91749, Net Wt. 1.5 oz."

During the 1860s the Yankee army came to Chestnut Grove and rode away with sides of bacon and Virginia hams. Just over a hundred years later the Yankees came back and left 1.5 ounces of apricot jam. I suppose that is progress.

"LIVING HISTORY" AND
KENNESAW MOUNTAIN

A few years ago, I first visited Kennesaw Mountain National Battle-field Park with thirty undergraduate university students—field trip—Sunday at the battlefield. One of the students in the class knew someone, I made some phone calls and did some coordinating, and our visit coincided with the dress rehearsal of the "living history" group at Kennesaw. On weekends during the spring and summer, volunteers dressed up in uniforms and period costumes and treated park visitors to demonstrations of Civil War weapons drill and camp life. So at Kennesaw, we saw not just the battleground, but also representations of how people lived in this place to which they came to kill one another.

Perhaps because the early spring was still cool and the sky slightly overcast, the park was not at all crowded. There was a sign restricting "ballplaying, sun bathing" and such frivolity. Nevertheless people come to Kennesaw to hike the trails, enjoy the green space, and to defy signs and drink beer in the sunshine.

Indeed, even as we assembled at the park Visitors Center, newsletters and letters to Congressmen were asserting that the park existed, in the words of one publication, "to commemorate a battle with memorialization and interpretation as its PRIMARY MISSION. It is not for picnicking, Frisbee throwing, kite flying, smooching on a blanket, etc., etc." Of course on this afternoon, at least, we had come to Kennesaw in search of history, because of what had happened here before Frisbees.

Before I arrived at the park, I had a textbook knowledge of what happened at Kennesaw on June 27, 1864. The action was, in one sense, fairly simple. Union General William T. Sherman confronted ten miles of trenches held by Joseph E. Johnston's Confederates and attempted a frontal assault designed to break through the Southern line. Sherman wrote his wife on the day before the battle:

> We have worked our way forward until we are in close contact—constant skirmishing and picket firing. He [Johnston] is afraid to come at us, and we have been cautious about dashing against his breastworks. My lines are ten miles long and every change necessitates a large amount of work. Still we are now all ready and I *must* attack direct or turn the position. This is Sunday and I will write up all my letters and to-morrow will pitch in at some one or more points.

Sherman concentrated his efforts and hopes at two supposedly weak points in the Southern line while maintaining some pressure everywhere. The attack quickly became a disaster, however, as Southern artillery and entrenched infantry mowed down the advancing Federals. By noon it was over. Sherman lost 3000 men and realized he would have to outmaneuver Johnston, rather than run over him.

The "living history" folks were authentic and enthusiastic. Members of the class and I learned the crew assignments for firing a Civil War artillery piece. We inspected the camp of some "Yankee soldiers" and watched two of them shoot muzzle-loading rifles. We visited the camp of the female "camp followers" (who insisted they portrayed wives and mothers of the soldiers), saw them cook corn bread over an open fire, and tasted the results. Then we went up to the top of Kennesaw Mountain and spoke with the "Rebels" who were encamped there. Class members really enjoyed seeing history "live," and the volunteers certainly added an extra dimension to the site.

We left "living history" and went with the park historian to the scene of some of the bloodiest fighting on that June morning in 1864. This part of the field was called Cheatham Hill, and here 16,000 men, roughly

Looking east from Burnt Hickory Road, Little Kennesaw at the left, Pigeon Hill at the right. Photographed a few days after Union troops moved across the foreground and attacked the Confederates on Pigeon Hill. Courtesy of the U.S. Army Military History Institute.

In Kennesaw Mountain National Battlefield Park today. Courtesy of Kennesaw Mountain National Battlefield Park.

8,000 from each army, confronted each other. First we examined some of the earthworks that composed the Confederate battle line. These works ran along the crest of the hill and from them we looked down the slope across open ground to a small level field. Beyond the field was a creek and some woods and that was where the Federals had formed for their attack.

The park historian asked if we would like to get a feel for what it had been like for those who made the attack. That sounded like fun, so we all walked down the hill and across the the small field to the tree line. There we formed a line and practiced trying to keep the line straight while we walked.

In 1864 the Federals had all but announced their intentions with an artillery barrage that sent the Confederates scurrying to those trenches at the crest of the hill. "Hell had broke loose in Georgia, sure enough," one of the Southerners remembered. Our day was cool; theirs was hot, probably 100° F or more. We wore jeans and carried nothing; they wore wool and bore the impediments of war. One of the Federal commanders, General Dan McCook who had been Sherman's law partner, recited a poem to his troops while they formed their assault line; our "commander" reminded us to keep our line straight.

"Quick time, march!" came the command, and we began to walk briskly toward the hill. As we walked, the park historian announced that the Southerners had opened fire. Still he admonished us to keep our line straight. We tried.

At the base of the hill which looked much longer and steeper from this vantage point, the park historian commanded, "Double time, march!" We began to run and our line became very ragged. Some of the panting students gratefully became "casualties" and tumbled to the ground. The rest of us kept running up the hill toward the trench line.

Just as the young man in the lead neared the trench, the park historian called, "Stop! Freeze! Don't anyone move." Then he asked us to look around. When we did, we saw that we were spread all over the hillside. Then he informed us that we were all dead. The soldiers in the trench would have had very little difficulty shooting us down, because we were in groups of two and three and very scattered. Only if we had kept our line straight and reached the trench line together, would we have had any chance to survive or succeed in our charge.

The Union troops whose attack we had just emulated were veterans; they were trained to keep their line straight, and they had done so many times in the face of enemy fire. Still, one of them remembered the "trenches were veritable volcanos—vomiting forth fire and smoke, and raining leaden hail in the face of the Union boys." Another wrote, "The air seemed filled, with bullets, giving one the sensation experienced when moving swiftly against a heavy rain or sleet storm." For reasons much more real, their line broke as ours had done. Many of their attackers fell down or fell back before the murderous fire.

But some of them reached the very edges of the Southern trenches where I now stood. A color bearer got this far and waved the "Stars and Stripes" in the faces of the Confederates. One of them yelled, "Look at that Yankee flag—shoot that fellow—snatch that flag!" Then an officer sprang out of the trench and wrestled the bearer for his flag. The color bearer managed to kill the officer just moments before he was himself shot. He fell tangled in the folds of his flag.

When the assault finally broke up, some of the Federals remained where they were in front of the Confederate trenches. Most of them withdrew. One of the Southerners recalled:

When the Yankees fell back and the firing ceased, I never saw so many broken down and exhausted men in my life. I was sick as a horse, and as wet with blood and sweat as I could be, and many of our men were vomiting with excessive fatigue, over exhaustion, and sunstroke; our tongues were parched and cracked for water, and our faces blackened with powder and smoke, and our dead and wounded were piled indiscriminately in the trenches.

For three long, hot days the armies faced each other in the wake of the abortive attack on June 27.

For three days the dead remained where they fell. Finally the stench of death became overwhelming, and the rival armies arranged a truce to bury the swollen corpses. Living soldiers bent bayonets into hook shapes and used them attached to their rifles to stay as far as possible from the smell while they dragged their dead comrades to mass graves. Soon after they completed this grim labor, the soldiers left this place. Sherman began to maneuver around Johnston, so on July 2 Johnston withdrew from his Kennesaw Mountain line and drew another closer to Atlanta.

The "charge" of the students and me up Cheatam Hill had been fun, and we learned lessons we could not have understood as well in a classroom. We had lost ourselves in some minutes of "living history."

But then and since I have asked, "Why?" Why did the Union troops line up and march, walk(!), into a "leaden hail?" And why did men kill each other over possession of a piece of colored cloth?

A very different generation of Americans fought at Kennesaw. They may have been braver or more foolish, but they seemed less impressed with death than we. In our time we seem to be more concerned for life and for individuals. In that time they were concerned for causes, and they responded to causes with greater discipline than would seem possible now.

Herman Melville spoke eloquently for the Civil War generation even while the conflict remained a current event. Melville responded to the Battle of Kennesaw Mountain with a poem:

On Sherman's Men
who fell in the Assault of Kenesaw Mountain, Georgia.

THEY said that Fame her clarion dropped
Because great deeds were done no more—
That even Duty knew no shining ends,
And Glory—'twas a fallen star!
But battle can heroes and bards restore.

"Living History" and Kennesaw Mountain

Nay, look at Kenesaw!:
Perils the mailed ones never knew
Are lightly braved by the ragged coats of blue,
And gentler hearts are bared to deadlier war.

On my way out of the park, I passed once more the sign about "ball-playing, sun bathing" and such activities some folks considered inappropriate here. Our "assault" on Cheatam Hill and my questions about the men who had made that attack "for keeps" were still fresh in my mind. Then I thought about the stench of the dead bodies, the bayonet hooks, and the mass graves.

Let the Frisbee throwers play; the kite flyers fly; and the smoochers-on-blankets smooch! They celebrate life in this place of death. And "living history" need not be a contradiction in terms.

TORPEDOES AND TIME
ON MOBILE BAY

"If you're not living in Mobile, you're camping out." So says the slogan on the cover of *Mobile* magazine and by extension says the Mobile Area Chamber of Commerce. Because I do not live in Mobile, I decided to do the next best thing—to "camp out" there for a couple of days. I went to see the site of the Battle of Mobile Bay that occurred in August of 1864.

My visit was hardly camping out. Ellen lived in a house that looks like an amalgam of *Town and Country* and *Southern Living*—with class. Inside were emblems of Mobile Mardi Gras Societies, antique furniture, mellow colors, and the ubiquitous chocolate Lab ("Buster Brown").

Early next morning I set out for the Bay. Mobile, city and port, lies at the mouth of the Alabama–Tombigbee River system at the head of the Bay that extends 30 miles to the Gulf of Mexico. At Mobile the Bay is 6 miles wide; at the Gulf it fans to a width of 15 miles. Mobile Point, a narrow, sandy spit of land encloses roughly half the mouth of the Bay on the east. Between Mobile Point and Cedar Point, on the west, is Dauphin Island. Smaller islands between Dauphin Island and the two headlands define channels that permit boats to pass to and from the Bay and Gulf. The main ship channel lies between Dauphin Island and Mobile Point, and that was where the battle took place.

Mobile Bay in 1864 was an enticing prize for the Federals to capture and a vital port for the Confederates to retain. By that time Mobile was the last major port in Southern hands on the Gulf of Mexico and was, with Charleston and Wilmington, one of only three significant ports available anywhere to the Confederacy. To defend the Bay, the Confederates relied upon a series of forts and obstructions that covered or closed the various entrances. Until 1864 the Union navy had been sufficiently impressed with the Southern defense system not to test it seriously. The Confederates had been able to bar the Bay to Federal warships, and at the same time keep it open to any blockade runners able to slip past the persistent squadron of Union vessels on guard off shore.

Beginning in January, 1864, the United States Navy put men and ships in motion to challenge the status quo on Mobile Bay and thus close the port to the Confederates. In charge of the operation was Rear Admiral David Glasgow Farragut. Born near Knoxville, Tennessee, in 1801, Farragut had lived 53 of his 62 years in the service of the navy, and began the experience of independent command at age 12 when he took charge of a prize ship captured during the War of 1812. In this war he was already famous for his capture of New Orleans in April of 1862. From New Orleans Farragut had suggested an assault on Mobile to the Navy Department, but at the time both he and his superiors determined that opening the Mississippi River took priority over closing Mobile Bay. Thus Farragut had fought the southern portion of the Vicksburg–Port Hudson campaign, and now returned his attention to Mobile after almost two years on "brown water." Farragut began planning in New York where he had taken a well-deserved furlough for himself and had taken his flagship the *Hartford* for refitting. He set sail south in the midst of a snowstorm on January 5, 1864, and twelve days later the *Hartford* anchored in the relative balminess of Pensacola Bay.

At Pensacola Farragut added significantly to what he knew about the Confederate defenses of Mobile Bay. Even before he left New York, however, he learned two important facts about his enemies in the impending operation. The Confederates had a new ironclad ram, the *Tennessee*, which was supposedly "more formidable than the *Merrimack*," and the Confederates had Admiral Franklin Buchanan to command Southern naval defenses and the *Tennessee*.

Buchanan was a year older than Farragut and could count almost as many years of sea duty. The Maryland-born Southerner had gone to sea at age fifteen and in his mature years with the United States Navy had served as first Superintendent of the Naval Academy (1845–1847), gone to China and Japan with the Perry expedition (1852–1855), and commanded the Washington Navy Yard until the secession crisis. Buchanan first served the Confederate Navy as chief of the Office of Orders and Detail, and then in February, 1862, he assumed command of the navy defenses on the James River in Virginia. In effect the new command meant command of the armorclad *Virginia* (née *Merrimack*).

The first time the *Virginia* left her dock in Norfolk, Buchanan took her, not on a trial run or shakedown cruise, but into combat against Federal wooden ships. Buchanan presided over the destruction of the *Cumberland* and the *Congress* and in the process revealed the depths of his aggressive soul. After the *Congress* struck her colors, Federal land troops fired upon the small boat Buchanan dispatched to receive the surrender and render aid to wounded Union sailors. "Old Buck" was incensed. "Destroy that damned ship!" he bellowed and ordered hot shot poured into the *Congress*. Still not satisfied, he seized a rifle, went on deck, and began firing at the Federals on the shore. The Federals fired back and Buchanan suffered a bullet wound in the leg. Only after he had been taken below to his bunk did Buchanan display any concern that his brother was an officer aboard the *Congress*. McKean Buchanan survived unscathed—but no thanks to brother Franklin. I would say that the blood in "Old Buck's" eye had been thicker that day than the blood in his veins.

Buchanan recovered sufficiently from his wound to take charge of Mobile's defenses in the fall of 1862. The old man was a stern taskmaster, a strict disciplinarian, and to the core a fighter. But at Mobile, Buchanan encountered more than his share of problems securing the men and tools with which to fight. Originally he had hoped to scatter the Federal blockaders outside the bay and make an attempt to recapture New Orleans. As matters turned out, Buchanan had many more promises of ships than ships and had difficulty finding officers and crews to serve the vessels he did have. Delays and inactivity did little to soften "Old Buck's" gruff manner.

By February, 1864, Buchanan had only one ship fit for sea duty, the *Tennessee*. But quite a ship she was. A bit more than 200 feet long with a beam of 48 feet, the *Tennessee* was clad with 4-inch iron plates on her sides, and 6 inches of iron covered her shield and stern. Her turtle-like appearance disguised her offensive capabilities, a formidable ram on her bow and 6 Brooke rifled-guns. The *Tennessee* did have limitations, though. It was possible to jam shut the iron shutters that covered her gunports with a lucky or well-aimed shot. Her engine was small and thus the *Tennessee* was slow (6 miles an hour) and difficult to maneuver. Finally the chain that linked her tiller to the rudder and controlled the capacity to steer the ship, ran across an open deck and was vulnerable to battle damage. Buchanan and the *Tennessee's* commander James D. Johnston were aware of the potential danger of the exposed rudder chain, but neither believed there was time to remedy the problem. Resigned to the fact that he would have to face the Federals with only the *Tennessee* and three small gunboats, the Southerner was also aware that he needed to act quickly if he were to act at all. And nature seemed to join the conspiracy of forces that delayed him. To reach the lower end of Mobile Bay the *Tennessee* had to cross Dog River Bar, and to do that the ship had to draw 4 feet less water. To float a ship drawing 14 feet over a 10-foot bottom the Confederates constructed "camels"—wooden caissons, which could be flooded, and attached to the *Tennessee's* hull, and then pumped dry to lift the ship. The first set of "camels" raised the *Tennessee* only 2 feet and fire destroyed a second set when they were almost ready. Finally on May 18, more than three months after her commissioning, the *Tennessee* crossed Dog River Bar into the deep water of the lower bay.

On May 22 Buchanan prepared for action. He knew his chances were slim, but wrote, "Everybody has taken it into their heads that *one* ship can whip a dozen and if the trial is *not made*, we who are in her are damned for life, consequently the *trial* must be made. So goes the world."

Again, though, the fates frustrated Buchanan. He had to delay his attack on the Federal fleet, once because of bad weather, and once again because the *Tennessee* drifted aground at anchor. By the time the tide rose and the ram was again afloat, Buchanan had lost all hopes of surprise. Consequently he abandoned his plan to attack the Federals and resigned himself to counterattack.

While Buchanan fretted, Farragut, too, was having logistical problems. When the Union admiral arrived at Pensacola, he found "ram fever" rampant in the fleet; the *Tennessee* was far more lethal in the gossip making the rounds than she or any ship could be in the water. Although he did not succumb to ram fever, Farragut was indeed concerned about the *Tennessee*. He requested "monitors" (as all ironclads had come to be called) and waited long months for their arrival. At first Farragut feared the *Tennessee* would come out and attack his blockaders before the monitors arrived; then, as inactive time dragged he found himself hoping Buchanan would come and fight, if only to relieve the tedium. When his ironclads were ready, Farragut planned to force his way into Mobile Bay and battle the *Tennessee* there. For such an operation he could do nothing without monitors, and thus Farragut sat and waited and nursed a huge boil that symbolically developed where he sat.

The Confederates during June and July redoubled their efforts to prepare a proper reception for Farragut's fleet. They had driven piles and built or refurbished forts at the several entrances to the Bay. Clearly the most crucial passage was the main ship channel. To guard the channel the Southerners had two forts, a line of driven piles, and a torpedo (mine) field.

Fort Gaines was on the eastern edge of Dauphin Island; it still is. When I reached the fort during my excursion to the Bay, I was impressed with how wide the ship channel seems to be. But then I watched men in very small boats tonging for oysters around Dauphin Island and realized that large warships then and now could not navigate these shallow waters. The channel, as I could see by the markers, is narrower than it appears and is closer to Mobile Point. In the battle for Mobile Bay in 1864, Fort Gaines was not a crucial factor. I climbed about the fort for a time, had a look at Dauphin Island (which was only beginning to recover from Hurricane Frederic in 1979), and then boarded a ferry for Mobile Point.

The day was bright, the water calm, and the ferry ride a delightful half hour. In 1864 the Confederates had driven piles across much of the channel to obstruct the passage of ships. They confined the channel still more by placing what they then termed torpedoes (now called mines) from the edge of the piles to a red buoy only about 160 yards from Mobile Point. And on the tip of Mobile Point was Fort Morgan, the most formidable feature of the defense system.

During the trip from Dauphin Island to Mobile Point, I saw a number of red buoys, but they marked the current channel and not mined waters. Still, I imagined the deadly game played in this place during the summer of 1864. During the day Confederates tended their "field," replacing rusty or leaking torpedoes with new ones, while the Federals watched from a safe distance. At night Federal volunteers in small boats rowed among the torpedoes as much as they dared and disarmed as many as they could. Next day, of course, the Southerners returned to plant more explosives.

Fort Morgan remains a large pentagonal mass of bricks and mortar. It has been a fort for quite some time. In the War of 1812 it was Fort Bowyer; some of the Andrew Jackson's army occupied it in 1814 and drove off the British after the battle of New Orleans. The Confederates constructed Fort Morgan over the remains of Fort Bowyer and installed big guns. Whenever Buchanan toured the forts he exhorted soldiers about serving their weapons "to the death."

The Alabama Historical Commission now oversees activities at Fort Morgan and operates the site as a tourist attraction—something for people to do on a rainy day at the beach. In addition to the fort, the site boasts a museum and souvenir shop, picnic areas, a fishing pier, a boat ramp, the Commandant's Quarters restaurant and Blue Goose Saloon. Amid these distractions I somehow managed to sit on the beach and think about 1864.

Out there in the Gulf beyond that oil rig, Farragut waited impatiently as summer wore on and the monitors did not arrive. At long last, in July, the ironclads began to join the Union fleet, and Farragut was more than ready for them. He coordinated his proposed dash inside the Bay to coincide with assaults by the army upon the Southern forts, and on July 12 Farragut issued his attack order. "Strip your vessels and prepare for conflict," the order began, and in it the admiral ordered anchor chains and sandbags to be draped and piled respectively on the starboard side of each ship to minimize the damage from Morgan's guns. For some time Farragut had been "playing with blocks" representing his ships to determine the best possible order of battle. On July 29, in a supplementary attack order, he supplied the necessary details. The four monitors (*Tecumseh, Manhattan, Winnebago,* and *Chickasaw*) would pass nearest the fort and thus provide a screen for the wooden ships. Seven propeller-driven sloops of war (*Brooklyn, Hartford, Richmond, Lackawanna, Monongahela, Ossipee,* and *Oneida*), each lashed to a smaller gunboat (*Octorara, Metacomet, Port Royal, Seminole, Kennebec, Itasca,* and *Galena*), would steam into the channel between the monitors and the ominous red buoy that marked the torpedo "field." Farragut himself wanted to lead the way in the *Hartford,* but bowed to prudence in allowing the *Brooklyn* to be first because she had a "cowcatcher" rigged to her bow to ward off torpedoes.

Once inside Fort Morgan, the Union fleet would have to contend with the *Tennessee* and her escort of three gunboats. Buchanan decided to deploy his small force just inside Fort Morgan and thus to extend the gauntlet the Federals had to run.

During the first days of August both Northern and Southern seamen sweltered in the discomfort of battle stations in the Gulf coast heat. The Confederates on board the *Tennessee* had the worst of it because of the oven-like qualities of their iron vessel and because their admiral insisted that they wear full uniforms when on duty. On the Union side Farragut's prejudice against drinking water undoubtedly added to his discomfort when he mixed wine with August heat.

Only the arrival of the *Tecumseh* from Pensacola delayed the battle, and on August 4 Farragut committed himself even without his last ironclad. Then toward sunset on the fourth the *Tecumseh* steamed into sight, and both sides knew that Farragut's fleet would make its fight on the next morning's tide.

Weather conditions at dawn on August 5 were nearly perfect for the invaders. The tide was running full into the Bay and light air from the southwest promised to blow the smoke of battle toward Fort Morgan. At 5:30 A.M. the Federals began to move and one hour later the *Tecumseh* began the battle by firing on Fort Morgan. One hour after that, at 7:30, disaster struck the attacking column.

The *Tecumseh* at the head of the procession had run by most of Morgan's guns and encountered the *Tennessee*. As the Union ironclad maneuvered to attack the *Tennessee*, she passed inside the red buoy and struck a torpedo. She sank in two minutes. As she did, her commander Tunis A. M. Craven waited at the ladder for his pilot to ascend; he insisted upon leaving his ship last. The courtesy cost him his life. When the pilot reached the top of the ladder the ship disappeared beneath him. Craven and 92 others went down with the *Tecumseh*.

As the Tecumseh settled to the bottom, confusion reigned on the surface. Twenty-one crewmen from the *Tecumseh* managed to escape her and floundered in the water. From the *Metacomet*, lashed to the flagship *Hartford*, came a boat to rescue these survivors. On shore General Richard L. Page who commanded Fort Morgan shouted, "Pass the order not to fire on that boat; she is saving drowning men." Gunners on the *Tennessee*, too, raised their sights.

While this was going on, the leading Federal sloop *Brooklyn* backed her engine and sat dead in the water. The *Brooklyn's* captain was afraid he had strayed into the torpedoes and was attempting to alter his course.

A lithograph issued in 1886, from a drawing by J. O. Davidson, showing the entrance of the Federal fleet into Mobile Bay. The *Tecumseh* is rolling over and the Confederate ram, the *Tennessee,* is in the foreground. Reproduced by permission of the Museum of the City of Mobile.

In fact the *Brooklyn* was blocking the entire column of ships and making stationary targets of them all.

Farragut witnessed this chaos from the rigging of the *Hartford.* He climbed up the ratlines to see above the smoke and perched himself above the battle, tied to the after shroud so he would not fall to his death on deck if wounded. First he ordered the *Brooklyn* to go ahead. But a mix-up in signal systems aborted the order. Then the admiral determined to take the lead himself and ordered the *Hartford* to pass the *Brooklyn*. As the flagship maneuvered by the *Brooklyn*, someone reminded Farragut of the torpedoes that lay in their path. "Damn the torpedoes!" Farragut shouted down to the *Hartford's* captain, "Four bells! Captain Drayton, go ahead!"

With the admiral in the lead, the Union fleet proceeded through the channel. No more torpedoes exploded, and Farragut's audacity saved the day for his fleet. Once past Fort Morgan, however, both the *Hartford* and the *Brooklyn* had to survive attempts of the *Tennessee* to ram them. The Confederate vessel, though, was too slow, and consequently the Federals traded broadsides with the *Tennessee* and churned into the open waters of Mobile Bay.

The *Tennessee* returned to her position reinforcing Fort Morgan as the rest of the Union ships paraded past. Her gunboat escorts scattered before the invading fleet. The *Gaines* suffered critical damage and ran aground near Fort Morgan. The *Selma* surrendered after a fruitless attempt to outrun the *Metacomet*. Only the *Morgan* survived, and she did so only by quitting the fight and retreating into shallow water.

Except for the *Tecumseh* the entire assaulting force managed to run successfully past the torpedoes in the channel and the guns of the *Tennessee* and Fort Morgan. By 8:35 the *Hartford* was at anchor about four miles inside the bay, and very shortly thereafter members of the fleet who were not engaged in the pursuit of the Southern gunboats joined the flagship. Farragut had 17 warships on Mobile Bay. Casualties were many, and battle damage was heavy. On the *Hartford* alone, 21 bodies lay on deck, and more wounded writhed in agony below. At least, Farragut believed, this day's battle was over. While Federal sailors washed the decks and surgeons attempted to aid the wounded, the fleet's cooks prepared a second breakfast for the men.

On board the *Tennessee* Buchanan was in a quandary. Now that Farragut was on Mobile Bay in strength, the Southern admiral knew that it was only a matter of time before the Federals would invest the Confederate forts by land and sea. When that happened the *Tennessee* would become a ship without a port and thus doomed at best to be scuttled by her own crew. Essentially Buchanan had three options. He could steam out into the Gulf and wreak havoc among the wooden ships still on station there, he could remain under Fort Morgan's guns and wait, or he could attack seventeen ships with one. The first two options would delay the inevitable necessity to fight Farragut without altering the odds. Thus Buchanan paced and pondered for a while—probably to assure himself of the logic of what he wanted to do. Then abruptly he commanded the *Tennessee's* captain, "Follow them up, Johnston! We can't let them off that way!" "Buck" was going to have his fight then and there.

Then *Tennessee's* "charge" up Mobile Bay into Farragut's fleet was not quite like that of the "Light Brigade." Fourteen of the Union ships were wooden, and the Union ironclads were smaller than the Southern ram. Buchanan had enough fuel to steam for six hours, and the capability to do considerable damage in that time. Nevertheless, the conflict between the lone Confederate ship and Farragut's fleet resembled that between a lone buffalo and a wolf pack.

As the *Tennessee* bore down upon them, the Federal ships scattered. Then, as Buchanan set his course to try to ram the *Hartford*, the Federals converged. First the *Monongahela*, then the *Lackawanna* rammed the ram in efforts to sink her. Next the two flagships offered each other glancing blows and as they parted exchanged broadsides at a range of ten feet. Farragut again climbed into the mizzen rigging to get a better view of the action and from this position was close enough to the *Tennessee* to board her as the ships passed. Then the Federal ironclads closed on the *Tennessee*. The *Chickasaw* maneuvered beneath the stern of the ram and blazed away; a shell from the *Manhattan* actually pierced the *Tennessee's* armor, but did not penetrate the wooden timbers beneath the iron plating.

The Southern ship was unable to fire upon the *Chickasaw*, because a shell had jammed the cover of the stern gunport. Buchanan was helping serve the stern gun when the damage occurred, and he was assisting as a crewman tried to repair the port cover when a shot struck just above the port. Southern sailors collected the crewman's remains in buckets. And the admiral suffered a broken leg from a flying splinter of iron.

Shortly after this, one of the *Chickasaw's* shots severed the *Tennessee's* rudder chain, and the ram no longer responded to the helm. Captain Johnston took a hurried survey of the damage and reported to Buchanan. By this time the *Tennessee's* smokestack lay on her deck, and her steam was falling rapidly. Four of the six gunport covers were damaged, and repeated failure of the gun primers had severely limited the ship's capacity to defend herself throughout the battle. And Johnston knew no way to repair the rudder chain so that he could steer the *Tennessee.* All this he told Buchanan. The old man replied, "Do the best you can sir, and when all is done, surrender."

Johnston climbed back to the gun deck and soon concluded that the *Tennessee* was little more than a floating target for Farragut's fleet. Accordingly he struck his colors which by this time flew from the handle of a gun scraper. Then Johnston ordered the engine stopped and raised a white flag.

The Federal sloop *Ossipee* was bearing down upon the *Tennessee* when the white flag appeared, and although the Union commander William E. LeRoy ordered his engine reversed, the *Ossipee* bumped the *Tennessee.* LeRoy then dispatched a boat for Johnston who was his old friend, and met the defeated Confederate with a glass of ice water and the promise of "something better for you down below." Farragut was soon on the scene, and he quickly dispatched his surgeon to have a look at Buchanan's leg. Thus the battle for Mobile Bay wound down. The Federals completed their hold on the Bay on the morning of August 23

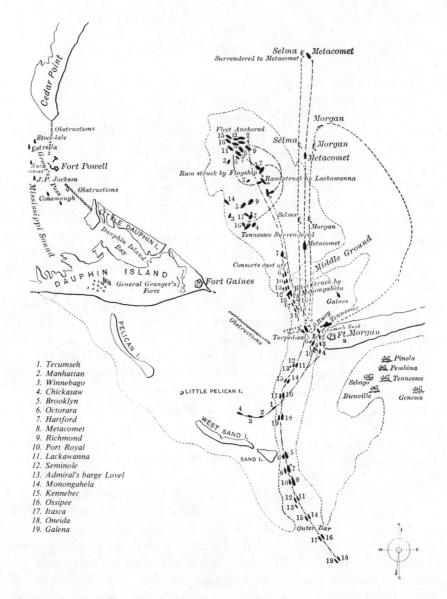

The Battle of Mobile Bay. Reproduced by permission of the Museum of the City of Mobile, this map is based on a diagram prepared by Rear-Admiral James E. Jouett.

when General Page surrendered at Fort Morgan. The Confederates there had followed Buchanan's example, spurned a suggestion to surrender on August 9, and held out until they were no longer able to return the fire of Union ships and land forces.

By the time I had rethought the capture of Fort Morgan and looked over the fort from the land side, I had had enough thinking for a while. I decided to indulge myself in a bit of nostalgia and return to Mobile by way of Gulf Shores, Alabama. Once upon a time I had indulged in some house parties with good friends near that part of the beach. We laughed a lot, played tennis, picked hard crabs, took naps, partied hard, fished poorly, sailed my Sunfish, and laughed some more. "The only thing like it was more of it, and the worst I ever saw was pretty good." Then some people moved, and our benefactor donated the beach house to Auburn University, and I had not returned in perhaps ten years. Now, nothing would do but to go to Gulf Shores and chuckle.

In the good old days I was recalling, our headquarters had been the Pink Pony Pub. A migrated Marylander named Vince ran the place and dispensed cold beer, hot gumbo, and his opinion of just about everything. And on the juke box Kenny Rogers vied with Neil Diamond. The Pink Pony in those days was also a haunt of then Oakland Raider quarterback Ken Stabler. A writer from *Sports Illustrated* once followed Stabler and his friend "Wickedly Wonderful Wanda" to the place and recorded: "The Pink Pony Pub dominates the beachfront of Gulf Shores, Ala., a resort-cum-fishing community south of Foley. A rickety stringpier extends into the Gulf of Mexico. Milky blue water laps the dunes of the offshore islands between Mobile bay and Pensacola. Girls in bikinis bake on the beach, turning slowly, voluptuously." The writer had it right. This was the spiritual center of "L.A."—lower Alabama, the "redneck riviera."

When I reached Gulf Shores and drove in the exit lane of a paved parking lot, I knew times had changed. There seemed to be more Volvos than pickup trucks, and lots of "Let me tell you about my grandchildren" bumper stickers.

The Pink Pony Pub still dominates the beachfront, but only because it sits closer to the Gulf than the rest of the structures on the high rise strip. Hurricane Frederic took away most of the rickety string-pier and forced some radical remodeling upon the Pink Pony. Vince was gone—to Florida they said. The gumbo was good; but the place was awfully sturdy, and there seemed to be yuppies about. "Milky blue water" may have been lapping between Mobile Bay and Pensacola. However neither I nor anyone else would see much of it because of the forest of condominiums already up and under construction up and down the beach.

The writer from *Sports Illustrated* had described local residents as of two types: "upper crust matronly, Rotarian, with cash register eyeballs" and "the Stabler gang, raffish, sunburnt, hard of hand and piratical of glance." Now, it seemed, those two sorts of people had mated and produced a new generation of raffish Rotarians, pirates with cash register eyeballs, and hard-handed matrons. "L.A." was big bidness. The "redneck riviera" had gone Sun Belt.

Alone on the road once more, I had little to do but muse about Mobile. I recalled my visit with Ellen—sitting among the trappings of Southern tradition discussing very recent American mid-life fads. I thought about Gulf Shores and the rapid transit from beach cottages to condos, from "good old boys" and "Wickedly Wonderful Wandas" to upwardly mobile young Americans and blue-haired nomads on the retirement circuit. Then I remembered the battle in 1864.

Confederate Secretary of the Navy Stephen R. Mallory wrote in response to the battle, "this contest possesses peculiar interest for all who are watchful of the progress of naval affairs, it being the first in which the modern and improved means of naval warfare, offensive and defensive, have been tested." Mallory referred to the extensive use of torpedoes, armorclad ships, and rifled naval guns. Never more would great power nations depend upon wood and sail on the seas.

Yet even though the battle for Mobile Bay was a case study in "modern" war, many of the actions and events of the operation were antique to the point of anachronism. After Farragut, admirals did not climb into their ship's rigging to observe battles, and most modern naval commanders have more respect for mines than to shout "Damn the torpedoes!" and order a course through a mine field. Rarely in recent times have combatants, in effect, called "time out" to allow rescue boats to save survivors of sunken ships. Since Buchanan, admirals have been more prudent than to attack seventeen ships with one and receive wounds while trying to help a common sailor repair battle damage. And recently victorious commanders in major sea battles have not greeted their vanquished counterparts with ice water and "something better for you below." The conflict on Mobile Bay was unique, not only as a harbinger of "modern" war at sea, but also as a vestige of antique actions and attitudes.

Then I realized that my entire trip to Mobile had been a study of time—of the paradox of modern war and traditional warriors, of the tension of living in the present with the baggage of the past, and of the persistence and pace of change in human experience. I had been "camping out" in Mobile. While there I had been struck by a heightened awareness that, like Farragut and Buchanan and all people, I was "camping out" in time—in that eternal moment when past confronts present.

PROTRUDING ENTRAILS
AND PETERSBURG

One June day in 1982 Kurt Vonnegut, Jr., the novelist, addressed hearers at the Cathedral of St. John the Divine and, later, readers of the *New York Times* upon the topic of nuclear peace. His words were surprisingly sanguine. One of Vonnegut's more intriguing reasons for hope is the state of modern communications—"the inventiveness which we so regret now may also be giving us, along with the rockets and warheads, the means to achieve what has hitherto been an impossibility, the unity of mankind. I am talking mainly about television sets."

"Thanks to modern communications," he contended, "the people of every industrialized nation are nauseated by war by the time they are 10 years old." Vonnegut suggested that television has made people aware that "war is meaningless butchery of ordinary people like themselves," and that "thanks to modern communications, Americans of all ages were dead sick of war even before we went into Vietnam."

Since we now know about war from viewing its horrors on television and since we also know that our potential enemies are "human beings almost exactly like ourselves," Vonnegut concluded, "the fun of killing enemies has lost its zing." "I bring you good news," he announced, "People have changed. We aren't so ignorant and bloodthirsty anymore."

I hope so. I would like to believe this "good news," and certainly Vonnegut's thoughts have a rational ring to them. But as I read Vonnegut's hopeful notion that since people now can literally see the horror of war, they will thus elect to avoid mass bloodletting. I could not help reflecting upon a photograph from the Civil War.

I first saw the photograph during a visit to the Library of Congress. At the time I was in search of some uncommon illustrations for a book, and I had the good fortune to encounter Milton Kaplan who then worked in the Prints and Photographs Division. Among the many items to which he directed me was a photograph of a dead Confederate soldier from the trenches of Petersburg.

Taken April 3, 1865, the photograph depicts a young corpse on what appears to have been a firing step or ledge of a muddy trench. He is barefooted; a hat covers his eyes and nose. His arms are folded behind his head almost as though he were stretching himself awake from sleep. An exploding artillery shell has torn away his stomach. His intestines protrude from a blood-soaked uniform and mangled flesh. Because the army to which the young man belonged surrendered only one week after his death, no one can convince me that his death was anything but meaningless. There are gorier glimpses of death among Civil War photographs than this. But this particular picture affected me immediately and has haunted me since.

Recently I visited the place where the young Confederate soldier died. Maybe it was morbid curiosity; I hope it was more than that. I would like to think it was respect for the young man's life and life itself that made me want to see where he died. Whatever the reason I went to Petersburg National Battlefield Park.

Before I went I did some homework about the fighting in which the young Confederate lost his life. The series of events that brought this man to that sodden trench near Petersburg began in late May of 1864 within the restless mind of Ulysses S. Grant. For the first three weeks of the campaigning season of 1864, Grant had pressed repeated attacks upon Robert E. Lee's Confederate army that defended Richmond. The Federal army attempted to flank their enemies by a series of forced marches to the east; but always the Southerners countered and continued to bar the way. In some degree of desperate frustration Grant or-

Thomas Roche's 1865 photograph of a Confederate soldier killed at Fort Mahone. Courtesy of the Library of Congress.

dered a direct frontal assault on Lee's lines at Cold Harbor on June 3. The ill-conceived attack proved disastrous, and during this single morning the Federals suffered 7,000 casualties. To this point Grant's campaign against Lee was a month old and had cost nearly 2,000 men per day.

So Grant returned to some thoughts he had been thinking before Cold Harbor and determined to make a bold move. On June 12 elements of the Union army began moving south to the James River, and by the next day the entire army had "disappeared" from Lee's view. Vigorous cavalry patrols screened the movement and kept Lee ignorant of the whereabouts of his enemy's infantry. Meanwhile four Federal army corps reached the James and the longest pontoon bridge ever constructed to that time—2100 feet, as long as seven football fields. At the same time another corps arrived by water on troop transports, and together the Federal columns advanced on Petersburg.

Located 23 miles south of Richmond, Petersburg was important as a railroad junction. If Grant could seize Petersburg, Richmond (and Lee's army) would have only one rail line connecting the Confederate capital with the rest of the Confederacy. Petersburg was a crucial step toward reducing Richmond to a state of siege in which Grant might simultaneously strangle Lee's army and the Southern government.

Awaiting Grant's surprise stroke at Petersburg were a small contingent of Southern soldiers and Confederate General P. G. T. Beauregard. As enemy strength grew before him, Beauregard sent desperate messages to Lee describing the danger. Lee had to be careful, though. He had to make sure that the threat to Petersburg was real before he committed the bulk of his army to meet it; otherwise he would expose the army and Richmond to destruction.

On the morning of June 16, Lee responded to one of Beauregard's dispatches, "I do not know the position of Grant's army and cannot strip the north bank of James River. Have you not force sufficient?" That afternoon Lee asked Beauregard, "Has Grant been seen crossing James River?" Soon after Beauregard received Lee's telegram, Grant attacked his 14,000 Confederates with three Federal corps (48,000 men). Somehow the Southerners held.

By June 18, Lee realized that Grant's army was indeed menacing Petersburg. But while Lee's divisions marched to Beauregard's aid, Grant threw 95,000 troops against Beauregard's 20,000. Again the Confederates stood their ground and finally Lee's reinforcements began arriving in strength. Miraculously, Petersburg remained in Southern hands, and Grant's masterstroke miscarried. Before Petersburg Grant paid for his costly campaign of constant marching and repeated frontal assaults. His men remembered Cold Harbor and so confronted Beauregard's defensive works with a contagious lack of enthusiasm.

At Petersburg the war in Virginia ground into immobility. Indeed it ground into the ground as both sides dug trench networks, earthern forts, redoubts, and redans, and constructed bombproofs, chevaux-defrise, abatis, and other devices designed to insure inertia.

The armies remained in trenches before Petersburg all summer, all fall, and all winter. In mid-January a young officer wrote to his father, "When we look at the thing in the abstract does it not seem foolish that two nations should sit down and dig, and dig again and sit down for eight long months in front of each other?" The trench stalemate may indeed have been foolish; but neither side could find a way to break it. Grant realized that he had run Lee "to ground" and that he could win a war of attrition. Lee realized that his army, reduced to about half the size of his enemy, could not survive outside of the trench network that evened the numerical disparity.

As spring approached in 1865, Grant began extending his lines southwest of Petersburg. He reached for another rail line, the loss of which to Lee would render Petersburg and thus Richmond untenable. Beyond the fixed fortifications marched 16,000 Federal infantrymen and rode 12,000 blue cavalry troopers. To counter this thrust Lee sent George Pickett with two infantry divisions and Fitz Lee's cavalry, a combined strength of 19,000 men. Pickett attacked a portion of the Federal force on March 31 and drove them back. Then on April 1 led his troops to a place called Five Forks and formed a defensive line.

Five Forks was and described a juncture of five roads that lay squarely between the Federal force and the railroad. However, Pickett assumed that he was safe for the moment and deployed his troops with little care.

During the late morning of April 1 Pickett and Fitz Lee both received some good news. Tom Rosser, who commanded some of Fitz Lee's horsemen, had been on the nearby Nottaway River, and the shad were running. Rosser himself had borrowed a seine and filled it many times. Now he intended to take advantage of the presumed respite and have a "shad-bake." Naturally Rosser invited Pickett and Lee to join the feast.

Just after midday Pickett and Lee left their commands without re-vealing where they were going and rode about two miles to Rosser's headquarters. There the split shad were broiling on sticks stuck into the ground before a hot fire. The men ate leisurely and perhaps passed a bottle about, too. At sometime during the extended lunch, two of Ros-ser's pickets rode to the headquarters and reported a general advance of the enemy along the roads they were watching. Yet no one heard any gunfire and in the absence of any more reports, the generals concluded that there was no cause for alarm. So the shad-bake continued.

Between four and five o'clock Pickett dispatched two of Rosser's men as couriers to Five Forks with a message for his command. The two horsemen had barely left the campsite when those still gathered about the cooking fires heard lots of small arms fire very nearby. They looked up and into a line of Federal infantry advancing in earnest against a ner-vous few Confederate cavalrymen. The party ended abruptly.

Pickett scrambled aboard his horse and dashed off toward Five Forks. He made his escape from Rosser's camp at considerable peril to his life, but he never reached Five Forks. By this time the Federals held the road juncture, and Pickett's troops were in full flight.

While Pickett was leisurely plucking small bones from his shad, his enemies advanced boldly toward Five Forks. Southern officers sent mes-sages to Pickett, but none of the couriers could find him. Accordingly no one was in charge when the Federals attacked. The Confederate left was the weakest portion of the Southern line and by chance the target of the heaviest Northern attacks. But no one on the Southern side was in a posi-tion to shift troops to the most threatened sector of the field. Conse-quently defeat became a disaster. Most of the Southern cavalry escaped; most of Pickett's infantry did not. The Federals captured about 5,000 Confederates on that April Fool's Day, and finally stretched Lee's lines to a breaking point.

On April 2 Grant's troops began a general attack along the long line

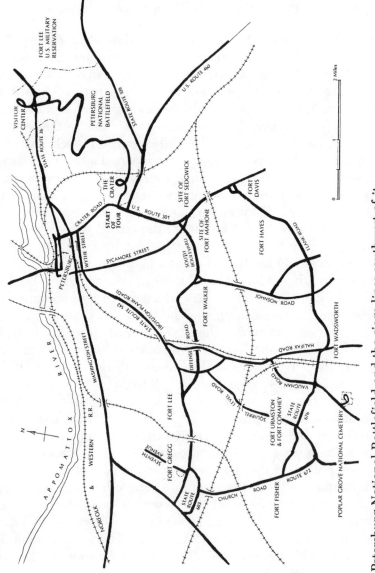

Petersburg National Battlefield and the siege lines southwest of it.

of trenches. The dead Confederate in my photograph was among the Southerners stationed at Fort Mahone, known as Battery 29 on military maps—also known as Fort Damnation to the men who garrisoned the place. It was a small place, mounds of earth and holes in the earth reinforced with wood, which protected a regiment of infantry and three artillery pieces. On April 2, Union units from Fort Sedgwick (a.k.a., Fort Hell) only a few hundred yards away stormed Fort Mahone in overwhelming numbers. The Federals seized the place and maintained a tenuous hold on it for most of the day. However, the Southerners in adjacent trenches stopped their enemies' advance and pinned down the Federals inside Fort Mahone with artillery and small arms fire. During the late afternoon most of the Northern troops withdrew back to Fort Sedgwick and a Southern counterattack reclaimed Fort Mahone.

Federal successes elsewhere along the Confederate lines on April 2 impelled Robert E. Lee to abandon the trenches around Petersburg which his army had held for more than nine months. The Confederates left their lines, and with them Fort Mahone, during the night of April 2–3 and began the march that ended on April 9 at Appomattox.

The dead soldier in the photograph with some of his comrades and some of his enemies remained at Fort Mahone where he fell. On the morning of April 3 photographer Thomas Roche, with his wagon and his assistant, followed the wake of the general Federal advance and stopped at Fort Mahone. For a few hours Roche and his assistant were the only live people on the scene. The Confederates had left, the Federals followed, and the burial details had not yet arrived to dispose of the corpses. Roche took twenty-two photographs of dead men that day. And among these photographs was the one which I had seen at the Library of Congress. All this and more I learned from William A. Frassanito (*Grant and Lee: The Virginia Campaigns, 1864-1865*), who has studied Civil War photography creatively and definitively.

At Petersburg I visited the battlefield park and saw the remains of "The Crater" which had resulted from an unsuccessful Union attempt to blast a way through the Confederate trench lines. A mine and 8000 pounds of gunpowder did blow up the Southern works; but the subsequent assault by Northern foot soldiers failed to exploit the advantage.

The site of Fort Mahone lies outside the boundaries of the battlefield park. However, the ranger's map and directions were easy to follow. The Fort was located at what is now the intersection of Crater Road (U.S. 301), South Boulevard, and Sycamore Street. This is a very active intersection. The Walnut Mall is there, and over where Fort Sedgwick was is a Sears store.

Where Fort Mahone was once is now a Uniroyal tire store. The only indication that this ground had not always been smooth and coated with asphalt was a monument/statue of a Civil War soldier. That soldier, however, is a Federal colonel who fell in the fight for Fort Mahone at age twenty-five.

As I left I reflected upon Kurt Vonnegut and photographs and wars. The American Civil War was really the world's first photographed war. When people could see such gruesome sights as the dead Confederate (instead of those quaint lithographs that portrayed battle as straight lines of colorfully dressed men led by other men on white horses), they should have recoiled and gone to great lengths to deter war. But such has not been the case; Americans have committed themselves to five wars since that young Confederate "posed" for the photograph.

But the story gets even worse. As Milton Kaplan explained to me in the Library of Congress, the original photograph was a stereograph or stereo. Thomas Roche took, not one, but two, exposures of the dead man from slightly different angles. The two exposures when blended and viewed through a hand-held device called a stereoscope, achieve a striking three-dimensional effect. The stereo reproduction of the Confederate corpse viewed through a stereoscope render the young man's protruding entrails especially vivid.

Oliver Wendell Holmes, the poet and essayist, responded to a collection of stereo views of dead bodies at Antietam in a way worthy of Kurt Vonnegut. "It was so nearly like visiting the battlefield to look over these views," Holmes wrote, "that all the emotions excited by the actual sight of the stained and sordid scene...came back to us, and we buried them in the recesses of our cabinet as we would have buried the mutilated remains of the dead they too vividly represented....The sight of these pictures is a commentary on civilization such as the savage might well triumph to show its missionaries."

The "death studies" of Antietam from which Holmes recoiled were more than a "stained and sordid scene." They were also a large commercial success for the firm belonging to Mathew Brady that displayed the photographs and then reproduced and marketed the prints. Undoubtedly the Antietam stereos inspired Roche to take his twenty-two stereos, including that of the dead Confederate soldier. Roche turned over the results of his labors to E. & H. T. Anthony & Co. in New York, and they reproduced the stereos and sold them to the public.

It is impossible to know how many people have stared at the body of the dead young Rebel. Once upon a time a stereoscope and a basket of stereoscopic views were all but fixtures in American homes. Indeed an observer of American life once ventured, "I think there is no parlor in America where there is not a Stereoscope." That solid citizens of the nineteenth century should purchase a copy of the Roche stereo and keep the view in their parlors to delight and amuse Sunday callers seems to me at least macabre.

It is also a pretty sad commentary upon human sensitivity. Michael J. Arlen who has pondered deeply upon the impact of Vietnam and television (*The Living-Room War*), suggests that combat scenes seem less "real" in part because of the "physical size of the television screen, which ...still shows one a picture of men three inches tall shooting at other men three inches tall, and trivialized, or at least tamed, by the enveloping cozy alarms of the household." Arlen may have a point; but that point does not apply to Civil War stereos; they fill the field of vision and offer a sense of depth which television screens do not. After more than a century, the dead Confederate's large intestine is all too "real."

The Crater as it appeared soon after the fall of Petersburg in 1865. Courtesy of the National Archives and *Civil War Times Illustrated*.

The Crater as photographed by Flournoy in the 1960s. Courtesy of the Virginia Chamber of Commerce and *Civil War Times Illustrated*.

A long time before television, people had graphic evidence that "war is meaningless butchery of ordinary people like themselves." That the dead young soldier and his three-dimensional entrails became items of entertainment only adds obscenity to object lesson.

Kurt Vonnegut is a gentle human being. I relish the zany iconoclasm of his novels; I wish I could share the optimism of his "good news" that, "We aren't so ignorant and bloodthirsty anymore." But the human experience of history seems to show that if we are to survive, to avoid nuclear holocaust, we must do something more than watch television.

PEACE AT BENNETT PLACE

At Gaffney, South Carolina, on I 85 is a water tower shaped like a giant peach, in recognition of the number and quality of peach orchards in this region of the Carolina upcountry. In 1981 "The Peach" won for Gaffney what I am sure is a highly coveted crown, the Water-Tower-of-the-Year Award. A unique structure it is. And perverse-minded passers-by have suggested that The Peach, viewed from the correct angle, resembles nothing so much as a monstrous human posterior. Peachoid—Carolina "moon"—or whatever, the water tower is a rare instance of roadway art that reduces Burma Shave signs to second-rate trivia.

Beyond The Peach, I 85 is a very mundane road. I drove it to get to Bennett Place which is very near Durham, North Carolina. There on April 26, 1865, Confederate General Joseph E. Johnston surrendered his army to Union General William T. Sherman.

Although this surrender involved more troops (89,270) than any other Civil War capitulation, Bennett Place suffers by comparison with Appomattox where Robert E. Lee surrendered to Ulysses S. Grant seventeen days earlier. I had been to Appomattox, and surely it is a poignant and powerful place. But I went to Bennett Place to contemplate the end of the war, because I believed (and still do) that the Johnston–Sherman negotiations were more important than those of Lee and Grant. What happened at Bennett Place, more so than Appomattox, made plain the issues that would condition peace and reunion. At Bennett Place, North and South confronted the fundamental question of whether the defeated South would be reconstructed—made over, constructed anew—

or resurrected—restored to the Union much as it had been before 1860–1861.

Bennett Place not only contributed to the end of the war, it also anticipated the peace. And the events and personalities involved in the surrender made a fascinating story. Somehow, Appomattox seems olympic; Bennett Place is more human.

The first thing I learned at the site was that Bennett Place (spelled with an "e") belong to Nancy and James Bennitt (spelled with an "i"). At the time of the surrender, military dispatches and newspaper reports regularly misspelled the name. So the North Carolina Division of Archives and History, Department of Cultural Resources, calls the surrender site "Bennett," refers to the "Bennitt" family, and, I am sure, tires of explaining the difference. Nevertheless it was refreshing to encounter a state agency more concerned with accuracy than bureaucratic consistency.

Indeed, the people who administer the site do an outstanding job. They have produced an excellent slide-tape presentation to introduce the events that took place at Bennett Place. They have filled just about every corner of the visitors' center with well-labeled displays relating to the surrender and to the Bennitt family. James Bennitt was a resourceful yeoman farmer, and a bonus feature of this historic site is an emphasis upon the lifestyle of people like the Bennitts. Visitors can see and appreciate not only the surrender story, but also the ways in which people who were not general officers lived in the nineteenth century.

Before the North Carolina Division of Archives and History, Department of Cultural Resources took charge of Bennett Place in the 1960s, the site was known locally as the "Surrender Grounds." People came here for picnics, and young people were known to use the place for "courting." In keeping with this tradition, those now in charge encourage picnics. Any "courting," however, must take place before 5:00 P.M., when gates close for the night.

On a Friday morning in October, the staff at Bennett Place outnumbered visitors. After I saw the slide-tape show and had a leisurely look at the museum displays, a member of the staff escorted me up a pea-gravel path to the reconstructed house and kitchen. He began a relaxed presentation by pointing out that pure accident brought Johnston and Sherman to this spot to negotiate surrender.

The circumstances that led the generals here to make peace began ironically in what was supposed to be a council of war. On April 12, 1865 (four years exactly since the first Southern gun opened fire on Fort Sumter), Joe Johnston met with Confederate president Jefferson Davis and members of his cabinet at Greensboro, North Carolina. By this time Davis directed a government on wheels—in flight from Richmond's fall and a general military debacle. Nevertheless Davis remained defiant and spoke of refilling the Southern ranks to continue the war. Johnston and most of the cabinet members who were present believed that Davis had lost touch with reality; but the president would not hear discouraging words and adjourned the meeting. Later that day Secretary of War John C. Breckenridge arrived in Greensboro and confirmed the rumor that Lee and his Army of Northern Virginia had surrendered three days earlier.

Next morning (April 13) Davis conferred again with his Cabinet and then summoned Johnston and General Beauregard to discuss the military situation. The remnant Army of Tennessee, which Johnston commanded, was still in front of Sherman's Federals as they marched through North Carolina; but the Southerners could do little more than flee in an orderly manner before the blue host. Johnston estimated that he then commanded an army of 25,000 men (actually he had less than 15,000) and faced a foe of 110,000 (actually about 90,000) under Sherman. The Confederate generals then made the obvious point that Grant and his Army of the Potomac were now free to join Sherman. The military situation was hopeless. Prolonging the inevitable would only spill more blood; it was time to make peace.

Davis did not like what he heard and said so. With great reluctance, however, he agreed that Johnston should ask Sherman for a general armistice "to permit the civil authorities to enter into the needful arrangements to terminate the existing war." Johnston sent his request for an armistice immediately to Wade Hampton who commanded his cavalry and instructed Hampton to send it through Federal lines to Sherman. Then Johnston left Greensboro and rejoined his army which was still retreating before Sherman.

In the morning on April 16, Sherman responded to Johnston's letter and proposed a conference to discuss the armistice. Johnston returned to Greensboro to discuss matters with Davis; but Davis by now had continued his flight to Charlotte, so Johnston decided to meet Sherman and make the best peace possible all by himself.

Meanwhile, as he prepared to meet Johnston, Sherman learned that he, too, had lost a president. He received the sad tidings of Abraham Lincoln's assassination. As soon as he recovered from the shock, Sherman ordered the news of Lincoln's murder suppressed; he feared that his army would respond with a vengeance frenzy and commence an uncontrollable orgy of death and destruction. Sherman carried concern about his men's reaction to the assassination in the front of his mind; in the back of the same mind was Sherman's conviction that many of his enemies would never quit fighting. He knew he could defeat regular Confederate armies. But in the aftermath of conventional conquest, he believed that Southern die-hards would take to the hills as guerrillas and continue the national anguish for another decade.

So Sherman wanted a speedy peace almost as badly as Johnston. The Federal commander hoped that Southern surrender would counteract any violent response to Lincoln's assassination. And he was prepared to make his terms generous in order to forestall, if not defuse, a very nasty partisan phase of this war. With these motives in mind, Sherman welcomed the opportunity to settle the war with Johnston and contribute something substantive to the peace.

So on Monday morning, April 17, Johnston and a staff entourage rode from Hillsborough toward Durham Station, while Sherman and his retinue rode from Durham Station on the same road. The generals happened to meet near Nancy and James Bennitt's farm and agreed to use the house as the site of their conference. Nancy Bennitt also agreed.

Of the small (three rooms plus a loft) frame house in which Sherman and Johnston met, only the chimney remains. The original structure and the separate log kitchen building burned in 1921. The State of North Carolina, however, has reconstructed these structures to look like sketches made of the originals at the time of the surrender. The generals met alone in the front room of the Bennitt dwelling. The Bennett Place staff has used a contemporary sketch of half of that room to recreate the furnishings. Even the smells (resin and wood smoke) seem authentic.

As soon as they were by themselves, Sherman showed Johnston the telegram he had received containing the news of Lincoln's assassination. Johnston agreed that this was very bad news, indeed. Then Johnston spoke of negotiations between "civil authorities," and Sherman balked. The United States recognized no legitimate "civil authorities" associated with the Confederacy and consequently he could deal only with men and matters military. Johnston countered with the suggestion that they, as generals, might negotiate a peace that encompassed, not merely their own armies, but the entire war. "With heightened color" (Johnston's observation) Sherman responded that they might just be able to do what Johnston suggested. The Federal commander believed he understood reunion as the primary Union war aim. He had recently had a long conversation with Lincoln on the subject, and these were extraordinary times.

Soon the two men were discussing details of the proposed peace. As Johnston had suggested, the discussion involved much more than the armies he and Sherman then commanded. They found much about which they could concur. However, Johnston wanted their agreement to include a general amnesty for all Confederates, including Jefferson Davis and his cabinet. Sherman felt he could not consent to this. He personally hoped that Davis and members of his cabinet would flee the country and so spare his government from having to decide whether or not to try them for treason. But he knew much better than to say such things publicly, and he feared that amnesty for Davis and his cabinet far exceeded his authority. But this seemed to be the only issue that divided the generals, and they spoke to it throughout most of the afternoon.

At dusk Sherman and Johnston agreed to resume their conversation at ten o'clock the next morning. During the night Johnston dispatched a telegram requesting Secretary of War Breckenridge to join him as soon as possible. The Southern general believed he was on the verge of securing peace from Sherman, and he wanted the support of his government. President Davis still pursued the dream of Southern independence, but that dream was clearly impossible now. Breckenridge understood that and would lend sanction to Johnston's pursuit of what was practical and possible.

Breckenridge arrived at Johnston's headquarters during the predawn darkness (April 18). He had Postmaster General John H. Reagan with him and together the two cabinet officers listened to Johnston's account of his session with Sherman. Then the three Confederates decided to prepare a written proposal for Sherman that contained the points discussed the day before, including the general amnesty. Reagan was still writing when it became time to set out for Bennett Place, so Johnston and Breckenridge left after making arrangements for Reagan to send his draft of the peace agreement after them as soon as he completed it.

Meanwhile Sherman announced to his men the news of Lincoln's assassination. Contrary to his apprehensions, the Federal army responded with shock and quiet rather than flames and mayhem. Sherman also spoke with most of his principal subordinates during that night and the next morning. They confirmed his opinion that the alternative to Johnston's surrender would be a "long and harassing march in pursuit of a dissolving and fleeing army—a march that might carry us back again over the thousand miles that we had just accomplished." So Sherman went again to Bennett House in the afternoon on April 18 still anxious to secure a surrender.

Once more Johnston and Sherman began their meeting alone, and again feelings were cordial. Outside Bennett Place, however, the men who accompanied the commanding generals were sometimes significantly less amiable. Rawlins Lowndes, who was a cavalry captain on Hampton's staff, had delivered Johnston's initial request for a meeting with Sherman. While he waited for an answer, Lowndes challenged Federal cavalry General Judson Kilpatrick to select 1500 men to meet Hampton and 1000 men, all combatants to be armed only with a saber. At an arranged signal the 1500 Federals and the 1000 Confederates would charge each other and "that will settle the question which are the best men."

Kilpatrick declined the challenge from Lowndes. But the Federal cavalrymen said that he would relish one more pitched battle with Hampton's horsemen. The last time they met, Hampton had surprised Kilpatrick's headquarters near Fayetteville on March 10. The Southerners had come in the dark and generated considerable consternation within the Northern camp. Kilpatrick himself had been in bed with a young woman who was not his wife and had had to flee the scene clad only in his shirt and drawers. Federal troopers eventually rallied and recovered their camps; but Kilpatrick still smarted from what became known as his "shirtail skedaddle."

At Bennett House, while Sherman and Johnston conferred, Hampton lay down on a bench in the yard. One of Sherman's staff described him as "bold beyond arrogance." Another spoke of his "vulgar insolence" and the "utter arrogance and selfishness which marks his class, and which I hate with a perfect hatred." For his part, Hampton roundly disapproved of the entire proceeding; he was not yet ready to surrender.

For a time on April 18, Breckenridge waited in the Bennitt yard with the rival staffs. Inside the house Johnston suggested to Sherman that they invite Breckenridge to join them. Sherman agreed only after Johnston agreed that Breckenridge would be present as a Confederate general, not as the Southern secretary of war. So Breckenridge the lawyer, the big Kentuckian who had finished second to Lincoln in the electoral college in 1860, entered the room chewing a large quid of tobacco.

Sherman greeted him, walked over to his saddlebags, took out a bottle of whiskey, and suggested that they all have a drink. He assumed, correctly, that the Southerners had not had much access to liquor of late. Johnston assented; Breckenridge seemed ecstatic. He spat his tobacco into the fireplace, rinsed his mouth with water, and poured what Johnston later termed "a tremendous drink." Then Breckenridge seized the stage. He waxed eloquent about the points Sherman and Johnston had discussed the day before and supported his views with precedents from several sorts of law. Finally Sherman protested. Who was surrendering to whom here?

Reagan's draft proposal of the peace agreement had arrived. Johnston read it aloud; then Sherman read the document to himself and pronounced it unacceptable—too "general and verbose." Animated by Sherman's whiskey, Breckenridge offered more legal language and examples in support of the substance of Reagan's draft. Finally Sherman sat down at the table and began writing. Johnston remembered that he wrote rapidly, so much so that the Southerner believed that he had come to the conference with the essentials of what he wrote settled in his mind.

Sherman did pause once in the midst of his composition. He went again to his saddlebags and took out his bottle. Breckenridge once again spat his chewing tobacco into the fireplace and anticipated an invitation to join his enemy in a drink. But Sherman poured himself some of the whiskey, put the bottle back into his saddlebags, and returned to his pen and paper. Soon he was finished, and he handed the paper to Johnston.

The Confederate general was more than happy with the seven points Sherman had written down. The agreement called for the armies to remain in place for two days, then for the Southern troops to disband and deposit their weapons and public property at their respective state capitals. State officers and legislatures were to take oaths as required by the United States Constitution to support the Constitution; having done so, those officers and legislatures would then constitute legitimate state governments. Federal courts were again to function in Southern states, and Sherman pledged that the United States would respect political and property rights of the former Confederates and not "disturb" anyone who lived peaceably and obeyed the law. In summary the generals agreed that the war would cease and a general amnesty would embrace the officers and men of all Confederate armies.

Neither Sherman nor Johnston had the authority to do everything involved in the peace agreement. Each pledged to seek the authority and carry out the provisions of the peace. When each commander had signed the agreement, the generals parted in the hopes they had ended the war and taken a long step toward reunion.

As the Confederate generals rode down the road toward Hillsborough, Johnston asked Breckenridge what he thought of Sherman. The Kentuckian first complimented Sherman's mind and will; but then he exclaimed that Sherman was a "hog"—"Yes, sir, a hog! Did you see him take that drink by himself?" Johnston suggested that Sherman had been intent upon his writing and thus simply forgot to offer the Southerners a second round. "Ah," Breckenridge responded, "No Kentucky gentleman would ever have taken away that bottle. He knew we needed it."

The armistice prevailed while Sherman's and Johnston's governments considered the agreement reached at Bennett Place. Meanwhile Wade Hampton responded to the peace terms by writing directly to his president. He was dissatisfied and said that he spoke for many officers and men within his command. "I am sorry that we paused to negotiate... no evil can equal that of a return to the Union." But members of the cabinet convinced Davis that Sherman's terms were better than they had any right to expect. So on April 24, a week after the first meeting at Bennett Place, Davis sent a message to Johnston that he would sign the agreement.

Very early the next morning (April 25) Sherman received a surprise visitor. Ulysses S. Grant had come in person to deliver his government's verdict. Grant's news was bad. President Andrew Johnson and his cabinet had rejected the peace agreement, and some Northern newspapers were all but accusing Sherman of having capitulated to the Confederacy.

Especially upset was Union Secretary of War Edwin M. Stanton. In fact Stanton fed rumors to the *New York Times* that Sherman had sold out his country and conspired to help Davis escape with the Confederate treasury. Stanton not only made sure that the administration quashed Sherman's peace; he had also ordered Grant to North Carolina to direct renewed operations of Sherman's army against Johnston.

Informed that Washington had turned down the peace agreement and that the war was about to begin again, Johnston relayed the news to Davis at Charlotte and asked for guidance. The Confederate president then telegraphed orders for Johnston to disband his infantry and to instruct the men to reassemble later at an appointed place and time. Davis also ordered Johnston to join the Southern government with his cavalry and as many other troops for whom he could find horses. Davis's orders were precisely what Sherman had feared; the Confederate president directed Johnston to inaugurate guerrilla war.

Johnston, however, decided to disobey the orders of his commander-in-chief and request another armistice and another meeting with Sherman to discuss surrender. The Southern general took care to tell his government what he was doing; in effect he announced his insubordination. At this point, Johnston believed "it would be a great crime to prolong the war."

Grant remained in Raleigh and sent Sherman to Bennett Place to meet Johnston and secure his surrender a second time. After all within the past year Sherman had defeated Johnston, then John Bell Hood, and then Johnston again. He deserved his moment.

They met at noon on April 26, and this time Sherman and Johnston did what Grant and Lee had done at Appomattox. The Confederate commander surrendered his army to the Federal commander. Southern soldiers signed paroles and promised not to take up arms against the United States. Officers and men retained their horses and private property. This time the peace of Bennett Place prevailed.

After Sherman and Johnston signed the agreement, they parted as close to being friends as was possible under the circumstances. A quarter-century later Johnston, who was 82 by that time, attended

A print copyrighted in 1876 by R. D. Blacknall, showing James Bennitt, who was 70 years old at the time, standing in front of his house. Courtesy of the Bennett Place, North Carolina Division of Archives and History.

Sherman's funeral on February 19, 1891. Although a cold rain was falling, Johnston insisted upon removing his hat and stated that if their positions were reversed, Sherman would have done the same for him. Soon thereafter Johnston contracted pneumonia and died.

In the meantime, Nancy and James Bennitt resumed their life at the surrender site. Both of their sons and their son-in-law had died during the war—perhaps as a result of the war. By 1875 James Bennitt was 69 and failing physically, so he quit farming and contracted with his in-laws to sharecrop his 325 acres. In 1878 James Bennitt died; Nancy Bennitt died in 1884. The Bennitt's grandchildren lived on the place until 1890, when they moved to work in the mills of Durham. So the Bennitt family not only took a very personal part in the collapse of the Old South; they also participated in sharecropping and mill towns, institutions that characterized the New South.

But what about the war which supposedly separated Old from New, not only in the South, but in the rest of the nation as well? What about the peace—two "peaces" really, one proposed and another established— negotiated at Bennett Place? What happened here in this unpretentious North Carolina farmhouse?

Sherman, for his part, believed he had been betrayed and identified Stanton as the betrayer. Two days after the surrender (April 28), Sherman wrote to Grant and gave him his views. He said of his enemies, "We should not drive a people into anarchy. . . ." And of his presumed friends he observed with bitter sarcasm, "It is true that non-combatants, men who sleep in comfort and security while we watch on the distant lines, are better able to judge than we poor soldiers, who rarely see a newspaper, hardly hear from our families, or stop long enough to draw our pay. I envy not the task of 'reconstruction,' and am delighted that the Secretary of War has relieved me of it."

Johnston, too, ended the war at odds with his government, and he subsequently devoted significant space and emphasis in his memoirs and correspondence to an indictment of the Davis administration. But Johnston also shared Sherman's contempt for the government of the United States. Enemy soldiers, Johnston believed, merely desired peace and re-union on the terms established initially at Bennett Place on April 18. And the conduct of the officers and men of Sherman's army inspired "a strong expectation that the Southern states would soon resume their places in the Union." In the wake of surrender, even "the most despon-dent [Southerner] apprehended no such 'reconstruction' as that subse-quently established by Congress."

Sherman and Johnston were warriors. Like many other men who had risked themselves in combat, they emerged from the conflict with greater empathy and respect for their recent enemy than for their own countrymen who had avoided active participation in the war. And be-cause they were warriors, they accepted the verdict of combat and per-ceived that verdict as the be-all and end-all of the war. The South had lost a war for independence; the North had won a war for Union.

But Sherman and Johnston and many others then and since missed the point of the peace. At issue was more than victory and Union. At is-sue was the very definition of the victorious Union. What kind of re-united United States would emerge from the peace? Would the seceded states of the South, in Johnston's phrase, "soon resume their places in the Union" and thereby turn back the calendar to 1860? Stanton and others said, "No," to this prospect. The long national trauma, the sacrifice of so much blood and treasure, and a martyred president demanded more than a return to "business as usual."

Most obviously at issue, and at the same time both the symbol and substance of Reconstruction in the South, was the fate of four million black freedmen. What began in 1861 as a "War for Union" became eventually a "Crusade against Slavery." At Bennett Place both Johnston and Breckenridge insisted that slavery was "dead," and thus Sherman did not include any mention of slavery or the new freedmen in his peace agreement. But even if slavery were no longer a factor, and the Black Codes and vagrancy laws soon enacted in Southern legislatures clearly revealed that it was very much a factor, crucial questions of race and class remained.

The sort of peace made originally at Bennett Place on April 18, in effect, consigned the four million freedmen to the tender mercies of their former masters and reaffirmed the class and caste system that had prevailed in the South before the war. At Bennett Place this issue, no less than the very definition of the Union, surfaced in substance. The difference between the April 18 peace and the April 26 peace involved much more than magnanimity versus malignity. The difference was resurrection versus reconstruction.

At that other peace place, Appomattox, Grant and Lee settled the war: North won; South lost. Bennett Place concerned the peace; by then the war was past; this event was about the future of the South and the nation. It left unanswered questions.

I left the historic site still thinking about war and peace and resurrection and reconstruction. And I reconfirmed my decision to think about these things at Bennett Place. Appomattox has a finality about it—a certainty that the great American bloodletting was over. Bennett Place underscores the ambiguity of human experience; it is a place of questions and paradoxes.

Sherman, the terrible scourge of the South, who contributed more than anyone else to the concept of modern, total war, was willing, even eager, to offer a lenient peace. Johnston, the cautious commander and for thirty-six years a career soldier, chose to disobey the last order he ever received from his commander-in-chief. Stanton, the irascible, devious politician who treated Sherman so shabbily in this instance, did understand what was at stake here and acted upon this understanding. How could Stanton be the hero and so villainous at the same time? And did Sherman really forget to offer Johnston and Breckenridge that second drink of his whiskey? Or was he protesting nonverbally the point that he, and not they, was the victor at Bennett Place?

By the time I had wrestled with these and more questions and contrasts, I was well down I-85 away from Durham. Indeed I was approaching Gaffney, South Carolina. Then did I realize that the paradoxes I was trying to resolve, the quandaries I considered, paled into absolute insignificance compared to the dilemma of some future archaeologist examining my present surroundings. What in the world will he or she make of the monstrous peachoid?

INDEX

Index

Index